The
CAPTURED HARVEST

The
CAPTURED HARVEST

Creating exquisite objects
from nature

TERENCE MOORE

PHOTOGRAPHS BY MICHELLE GARRETT

Trafalgar Square Publishing

NORTH POMFRET, VERMONT

To Suzy, Nicholas and William, who were
frequently banished to the far corners of the house
to let me make this book possible

First published in the United States of America in 1993 by
Trafalgar Square Publishing
North Pomfret
Vermont 05053

Copyright © 1993 Anness Publishing Ltd

Conceived and produced by
Anness Publishing Ltd
Boundary Row Studios
1 Boundary Row
London SE1 8HP

ISBN 0-943955-74-2
Library of Congress Catalog Card No: 93–60140

Editorial Director: Joanna Lorenz
Editor: Nicky Thompson
Designer: Peter Butler
Photography: Michelle Garrett

Printed and bound in Hong Kong

PAGE ONE
Topiary designs (see page 95), made by pinning
preserved oak leaves to a dry foam cone and ball.

PAGE TWO
From top left to bottom right: fir cone and moss tree (see
page 90); a mixed tied stack including carthamus,
echinops, nigella, larkspur and wheat (see page 141); a
triangular mossed garland (see page 115); an
experimental display of moss, cones and fungi (see page
123); a spring version of the Forest Candle Pot basket (see
page 44); a mini-swag for a Summer Table Setting (see
page 144); a Traditional Tiered Basket of roses and
larkspur (see page 70); a topiary variation on the Rose
Tree (see pages 78–83) made with protea and moss; a
variation on a garland for a spring table (see page 107).

PAGE THREE
A Sunflower Ring Extravaganza (see page 104).

OPPOSITE
A Grand Mixed Summer Pot of carthamus and nigella
orientalis (see page 31).

WARNING
In some of the displays in this book, candles form an
integral part of the design. Burning candles are beautiful
but can be extremely dangerous when used with dried
materials. It is recommended that candles be firmly secured
and that lighted candles never be left unattended. Where
feasible, electric candles may be used as safe alternatives.
In addition, effective flame-resistant spray may be applied
to displays, although this will not make them fireproof.

CONTENTS

INTRODUCTION

Until recently, the most usual alternative to a vase of fresh flowers was often a 'typical' arrangement of dried flowers – and this tended to be a few helichrysums and some sea lavender, bunched together in a somewhat uninteresting basket. All too frequently, this finished display would be left in a corner, where it would gather dust and be forgotten while its colours faded! However, in the last few years there has been a delightful and welcome trend towards much more innovative designs which make excellent indoor decorations. These striking displays of dried materials can sometimes be bought ready-made but they are usually very expensive and the range is limited – and of course it is much cheaper and more fulfilling to make your own. This book shows you how to do just that, creating stunning designs that will last for at least a year, and often much longer.

Always remember that displays do not have to be limited to flowers – some designs can also be a mixture of fresh and dried materials. Seedpods, fir cones, seashells or even pieces of driftwood are among the ingredients you might like to experiment with – unusual shapes and textures can make all the difference to a design. Most of the arrangements in this book are based on my favourite ingredients, but you may well have other items to hand that would look equally good in an arrangement. The key to success is not to be intimidated. If you are unsure about whether or not something is going to look good, the answer is to experiment to find out whether or not it works. However, do remember that it is all too easy to spoil a display by adding unnecessary ingredients or reworking too frequently. Knowing when to leave a display well alone is an acquired art which you will soon achieve with practice.

A few hints will help you to make the most of the projects in this book. Rather like learning to swim or to ride a bicycle, it is important to feel confident with the materials that you are using. The majority of materials are used dried. The exceptions are ingredients like moss and twigs, which are nearly always used fresh – in fact, the fresher

ABOVE
A moss ring (see page 101) is a useful alternative to a hay ring as the base for a garland. Here, the ring is not decorated with flowers but left in a natural state, tied with a wide fabric ribbon, which is wrapped a few times around the garland and finished in a large bow.

OPPOSITE
Even unwanted waste materials left over from a display can be put to wonderful use. This tree is made with trimmed larkspur stems in the same way as a Rose Tree (see page 79).

and greener they are, the easier they are to work with. Always remember when you are building up your display to plan your work so that delicate ingredients such as roses and peonies are the last additions to an arrangement. This will reduce any risk of damage to the flower heads, which is especially important as roses tend to be much more expensive than most other dried materials.

If you choose to buy dried materials, rather than dry your own, make sure that you only buy fresh stock and check that there are no signs of moths. When you first start making displays, you will probably be surprised at how much material you need – so start with smaller arrangements before moving on to larger, more ambitious projects. If you want to dry materials yourself, you will discover that some varieties are easier to dry than others. There are many drying techniques but the simplest way is to air-dry flowers and foliage by hanging them upside down in bunches, wrapped loosely in open-ended paper and in a dry, warm place. This works for the majority of plants, but a few cannot be satisfactorily dried in this way; for instance, ferns will become extremely brittle and very difficult to work with – though these can easily be purchased ready-preserved (or you can preserve your own), which saves much time and trouble.

Whatever type of arrangement you plan to create – from the simplest rose display in a terracotta pot to an abstract sphere of leaves or overflowing garland of flowers and foliage – remember that although this book contains all you need to know to make your particular display a success, there are in fact no fixed rules about arranging with natural materials, simply guidelines to help you. The most important thing is to read through the whole project before you start and give yourself plenty of time and space in which to work, so that you do not feel rushed or crowded. You will find that the more you experiment, the more fun you will have arranging your available ingredients. There is no limit to the designs you can achieve, so once you feel confident working with dried materials, feel free to adapt the ideas in this book which will, I hope, inspire you to create your own wonderful displays.

TERENCE MOORE

RIGHT
Occasionally, fresh materials can be combined with dry to great effect. This version of the Blue Pine Tree (see page 85) is decorated with bunches of cinnamon twigs, raffia and cones. Do not leave burning candles unattended.

POTS OF FANCY

POTS CAN BE FILLED WITH COUNTLESS MATERIALS: FIR CONES; SEASHELLS; MOSSES; ROSES; DRIED FLOWERS AND GRASSES; CREAMY CHURCH (VOTIVE) CANDLES. EVEN THE SIMPLEST CREATIONS CAN BE STUNNINGLY EFFECTIVE. EXPERIMENT WITH WHATEVER INGREDIENTS YOU HAVE TO HAND TO DISCOVER DIFFERENT COMBINATIONS.

POTS OF FANCY

Decorative pots are extremely versatile, making exquisite gifts, candleholders, table centrepieces or mantelpiece displays, perhaps arranged singly or in rows. From unadorned groupings of roses and herbs to elaborate combinations of woodland material, the techniques for creating pot displays are quite straightforward. Simplicity is the key to effective display work, as it is usually the least 'overworked' pieces that have the greatest charm and impact. Take great care to choose quality ingredients, and remember to balance the colour and textural elements in an arrangement.

Pots filled with flowers or foliage can be displayed in numerous situations. For instance, you could use one to decorate a patio table, alongside the food and wine. Or for a simple, striking effect, create a collection of pots filled with moss and large church (votive) candles for a dramatic indoor display. Sprinkle essential oil over the finished pots (avoiding the petals) for a wonderful long-lasting fragrance.

TERRACOTTA POTS

Antique earthenware and terracotta have a warmth and beauty that are hard to match, and which complement natural organic materials perfectly. When old pots are hard to find, choose good-quality hand-thrown pots wherever possible. If you leave them outside to weather for a while, they will soon become naturally distressed and acquire a rustic look. However, other containers (such as glazed china, or wooden boxes) can often equally well be used instead of pots.

PREVIOUS PAGE
Roses need not be used in complicated arrangements for them to create a dramatic effect. Here, two simple pots of roses (see page 21) sit delightfully beside the candle pot with perfumed roses (see page 25). Additional rose heads scattered around the pots link the displays together. Candles always provide a flattering light but take care never to leave them unattended.

FILLING A POT WITH DRY FOAM

1

This basic method is the same for the majority of pot projects and should be done with care. Try to work with plenty of clear work surface around you, and clean up any mess as you go along. First, invert the pot onto the dry foam block and press down slightly.

YOU WILL NEED
terracotta pot
dry foam block
knife

LEFT
When working with terracotta pots, it is quite easy to create a design with impact without using a multitude of materials. Here, deep orange marigolds are displayed on their own with only a covering of moss concealing the foam in the pot. Care was taken to ensure that the flowers were placed at varying heights (so they do not crowd or hide each other). Always try to match a display to its proposed environment. For instance, the colour of the marigolds works well here, set off against a mahogany box from India.

2

Lift up the pot to reveal the indentation made when you pressed down. Put the pot to one side.

3

Cut away the excess foam from the block with a sharp knife following the line of the indentation. Slice downwards through the foam at an angle, trying to keep to the rough shape of the pot.

4

Push the foam into the pot — it should fit snugly. If it is too big, cut off a little more foam until it is the right size. To minimize possible damage to the foam, turn the pot upside down and push on the base of the pot, thus easing the foam into it (rather than pushing with your hand directly on the foam).

5

Cut off any excess foam so that it aligns smoothly with the top of the pot.

MAKING A BASIC ROSE DISPLAY

1

Trim a piece of foam to fit the pot, and press down into the base so that it is set down a little below the rim (see page 13 for method).

2

Wire small bunches of 3–4 roses, ensuring that they are of even length (see page 150 on wiring). Press the roses firmly into the foam, positioning them quite close together and leaving an empty outer ring of foam.

3

Fix handfuls of moss into the foam around the flowers, with stub (floral) wires bent into U-shapes. The moss should neatly surround the roses and just cover the edge of the pot.

YOU WILL NEED
terracotta pot
dry foam block
stub (floral) wires
roses
moss
knife
cutters

RIGHT
Single-ingredient pots can be stunningly effective. Here a selection of plants have been displayed in individual pots: (top row) achillea ptarmica (The Pearl), oregano, and marjoram; (bottom row) carthamus and lavender. These pots would be very happy on a kitchen pine dresser, giving the illusion of growing plants. To create each mini-display, fill the pot with foam and then add wired bunches of each plant, following the same method as the rose pot on this page.

COUNTRY ROSE
POT

THIS POT OF RURAL ROSES HAS A
PLEASING DISHEVELLED APPEARANCE,
EMPHASIZED BY THE LAYER OF HAY
ATTACHED TO THE OUTSIDE OF THE
TERRACOTTA POT. IT IS TRIMMED WITH A
LARGE LOOSE RAFFIA BOW, AND WOULD
LOOK WONDERFUL ON A DRESSER OR
KITCHEN CABINET.

YOU WILL NEED
terracotta pot
dry foam block
reel (spool) wire
hay
red roses
poppy heads
stub (floral) wires
raffia
knife
glue or glue gun (optional)
scissors or cutters

LEFT
*To ensure that the roses keep their
colour, keep the display out of direct
sunlight. If the flowers or poppy heads
become a little dusty after a while,
brush them clean with a dry
paintbrush — or blow the dust away
with a hairdryer.*

1

Cut the foam block with a knife to fit the pot (see page 13) and press firmly in. Tightly wrap reel (spool) wire 2–3 times around the pot near the top; this is to secure the wire so that it does not slip when you add the hay. If you have a glue gun, you could glue the wire to anchor it firmly to the pot.

2

Lay the pot on its side and begin to wire on the hay in generous amounts. Do not worry at this stage if the hay is very uneven, because it will be trimmed later. As you add the hay, tightly trap it under the wire. If necessary, take the wire completely around the whole pot each time you add a new bundle of hay. This will ensure that none falls off.

When the pot is covered, tie the wire as tightly as possible. If you wish to be quite certain that the hay will not come off, glue around the pot over the wire and into the hay. Now trim the hay with scissors or cutters so that the base of the pot is showing. Pull off any loose strands of hay. Do not trim the top but remove any very long or straggly pieces. You should be aiming to get the hay looking fairly tidy, but do not spend too long fussing over it. The whole design will be transformed once you have started to add the flowers.

3

Separate the roses and poppies and wire them in groups of 3–4 into small bunches (see page 150), although you might find it easier to work with individual, single stems. The heads need to show above the top of the hay collar, so remember to leave enough length on the stems to push into the foam. Fill the centre of the pot with the roses and poppy heads, making sure that you have a good balance of colour and form. Finally, tie a raffia bow around the pot to cover the wire that is fixing the hay. Try to make the loops of the bow well rounded and generous in size. Trim any unwanted raffia from the ends as necessary.

ABOVE

This variation of the Country Rose Pot shows how easy it is to achieve a quite different feel simply by changing the colour of the roses. Here country-style ingredients create a pretty, casual display. If you like, you could also replace the raffia bow with a fabric or paper one for an instantly more sophisticated look.

EVENING CANDLE POT

THE MOST BASIC OF MATERIALS ARE USED TO GREAT EFFECT IN THIS SIMPLE-TO-MAKE CANDLE POT. YOU SHOULD BE ABLE TO BUY DIFFERENT COLOURED MOSSES FROM THE WIDE VARIETY THAT IS AVAILABLE OR YOU COULD USE NATURAL MOSS COLLECTED FROM YOUR GARDEN OR PERHAPS FROM A NEARBY WOOD. DISPLAY CANDLE POTS AT A DINNER TO ADD A SPECIAL ATMOSPHERE TO THE OCCASION — THEY CAN BE PARTICULARLY EFFECTIVE WHEN ARRANGED IN SMALL GROUPS. REMEMBER NEVER TO LEAVE BURNING CANDLES UNATTENDED!

1

These are very quick and simple to make. Fill the base of a terracotta pot with moss about halfway up. Do not bother to disentangle any twigs or natural debris from the moss — this is an unnecessary waste of time and, in fact, twigs tend to enhance rather than detract from the overall effect.

2

Stand a candle in the middle of the pot and then push more moss all around the candle. Press down firmly so that the moss is well compacted and holding the candle in place. When you get near to the rim of the pot, reduce the pressure so that the moss simply spills over the rim.

ABOVE

Here, a candle pot is displayed in an outside lantern, where it will greet visitors with a flickering welcome light for hours. The lantern itself is decorated with a garland of twigs and a fabric bow. Experiment with different types of moss for the pots: it is available in many dyed colours and even as a natural product comes in many forms. Good-quality moss can often be found on a woodland walk, and be especially attractive when mixed with a few fallen leaves.

YOU WILL NEED
small terracotta pots
good quantity of sphagnum moss
cream church (votive) candles

A SIMPLE POT OF ROSES

THE METHOD FOR THIS LARGE POT IS VERY SIMILAR TO THAT FOR THE SMALL ROSE POT SHOWN EARLIER (PAGE 14) BUT YOU DO NOT NEED TO WIRE THE ROSES INTO BUNCHES — INSTEAD CAREFULLY PLACE THEM IN THE FOAM ONE AT A TIME, MAKING SURE THAT THE ROSE HEADS ARE WELL SPACED TO CREATE A GOOD BALANCE. YOU CAN ADD ONE OR TWO OTHER VARIETIES OF DRIED MATERIAL TO THE DISPLAY, IF YOU LIKE, BUT IT WILL LOOK MOST EFFECTIVE IF THE DESIGN IS KEPT AS SIMPLE AS POSSIBLE.

WHEN USING ROSES ALONE IN A LARGE DISPLAY, STEAM THE HEADS OPEN A LITTLE WAY BEFORE YOU START WORK (SEE PAGE 150). BOUGHT FLOWERS OFTEN LOOK SQUASHED, AND AS THEY ARE SUCH AN IMPORTANT PART OF THIS DISPLAY THEY SHOULD LOOK THEIR BEST. FOR A REALLY STUNNING EFFECT, USE DIFFERENT COMBINATIONS OF SIZE AND COLOUR, AND TRY TO RETAIN AS MUCH OF THE GREEN LEAF AS POSSIBLE.

LEFT
A simple rose pot display can be made in single colours or, as here, with a combination. Roses work very well on their own but you could, of course, insert other ingredients for a different look. Make a matching pair to stand on a mantelpiece or shelf for a symmetrical, formal effect, or perhaps add a fabric bow for a softer, more romantic appearance.

1

Invert the pot and press to form an indentation on the foam block. Following the line the pot has made, cut off the excess foam with a sharp knife.

2

Trim the foam to fit the pot tightly and push in. ▶

YOU WILL NEED
terracotta pot
dry foam block
roses in colours of your choice
moss
stub (floral) wires
knife
cutters
glue gun (optional)

3

Press the foam firmly down into the pot; trim the top if necessary so that the foam and the top of the pot are level.

4

You will need about 30 steamed roses (see page 150). Trim each stalk to the required length as you work. In the finished display, the roses should be at different levels so that the heads do not obscure or crowd each other.

5

Start in the middle of the foam, pressing in the tallest rose. Then work outwards, continuing to add the stems one by one. Arrange the roses to any height, but make sure that they are a good balance for the size of the pot that you are using.

6

Continue to press flowers into the pot; if you are using more than one colour, ensure that you have a good mix of hues over the display.

7

Finally, fix moss around the base of the roses with a glue gun, taking care not to burn yourself on the hot glue. Alternatively, bend short stub (floral) wires over to form U-shaped staples which can be pushed into the foam to trap the moss.

RIGHT
The colours of these peachy-pink and yellow roses are naturally offset by the subdued green moss and terracotta. Wherever possible, try to use antique terracotta pots which have a pleasing texture and sympathetic look. If you can only obtain plastic pots, you can always conceal them in outer containers that reflect the colours of the displays.

CANDLE POT
WITH
PERFUMED
ROSES

THIS IS A DELICATE AND APPEALING DESIGN, BASED ON A FLOWER-FILLED HAY COLLAR THAT IS SECURED TO THE TOP OF A POT, LEAVING THE CENTRE FREE FOR A LARGE CANDLE. YOU COULD MAKE ONE FOR EACH TABLE SETTING AT A DINNER PARTY, OR ALTERNATIVELY MAKE A FEW LARGER POTS AS A CENTREPIECE, WITH VIBRANT GREEN MOSS AND SMALL FRUITS ARRANGED AROUND THEIR BASES.

YOU WILL NEED
small hay collar (see page 151)
terracotta pot
moss
roses
small-leaved foliage such as bupleurum
candle
scissors
glue or glue gun
cutters

LEFT
In these delightful candle pots, one shows a simple combination of pink roses and bupleurum, while the other is a mixture of large and miniature roses. With this version, add the smaller roses after filling the main gaps with bupleurum. Perfumed oil gives a wonderful lasting fragrance to the display; sprinkle a few drops of rose oil on the moss. Remember never to leave a lighted candle unattended.
CAUTION — Do not leave burning candles unattended.

1

Make the hay collar (see page 151) and measure around the inside rim of the pot before trimming its length to fit.

2

Glue the hay collar into place so that it is stuck inside the rim of the pot as near to the top as possible. Hold it firmly in position for a few seconds while the glue begins to harden.

3

Glue moss to the collar so that it also covers the rim of the pot. Now you are ready to start adding flowers.

4

Cut the rose heads from their stems, and glue them into place. Work from one side of the pot to the other so that you keep the flowers balanced. Make sure that the hole in the centre of the pot remains large enough to take the candle. After the roses, fill any gaps with greenery. Next, place moss in the base of the pot so that it half fills the pot. Press it down firmly to form a solid base for the candle to sit on. The aim is to have as much of the candle exposed as possible.

LAVENDER AND MOSS POTS

DIFFERENT TYPES AND SHADES OF
LAVENDER CAN GIVE VERY DIFFERENT
LOOKS TO YOUR PROJECT — THE DARK
BLUE LAVENDER HERE IS RICH AND
DRAMATIC ENOUGH TO WARRANT
DISPLAYING ALL BY ITSELF. YOU CAN, OF
COURSE, USE ANY VARIETY BUT THE
DEEPER THE COLOUR, THE MORE IMPACT
IT WILL MAKE. IF THE LAVENDER'S
POWERFUL SCENT FADES IN TIME, YOU
CAN EASILY BRING IT BACK BY ADDING A
FEW DROPS OF PERFUMED OIL TO THE
DISPLAY. ADD THE DROPS TO THE MOSS
AT THE BASE FOR BEST RESULTS.

YOU WILL NEED
lavender or herbs of choice
small terracotta pot
stub (floral) wires
dry foam block
moss
mossing (floral) pins (optional)
scissors
cutters
knife
glue or glue gun

LEFT
*Herb pots can be placed in most
interior situations, but avoid exposing
lavender in particular to too much
light. If displayed in a conservatory,
for example, the colour will soon fade.
Sunlight and damp are the worst
enemies of dried flowers!*

1

Trim the lavender stalks to length, so
that the heads will all come just above
the rim of the pot and the bunch is even.

2

Wire small bunches of 6–8 lavender
stems together (see page 150). You will
need about 3 bunches of this size to fill a
small pot.

3

Cut 3 small wedges of dry foam from the
block with a knife. Place one in the base
of the pot and gently push the lavender
bunches together into the centre. Then
press the other pieces of foam down
each side to hold the lavender securely
in place. The foam should be about ½in
(1cm) below the rim of the pot.

4

Glue the moss — any type is suitable —
into place over the top of the foam,
around the lavender. Alternatively, you
can fix the moss in position with mossing (floral) pins or short lengths of stub
(floral) wire bent into a U-shape.

WINTER
CANDLE POT

THIS WELCOMING CANDLE POT IS MADE
IN THE SAME WAY AS THE ONE WITH
PERFUMED ROSES (SEE PAGE 25) EXCEPT
INSTEAD OF THE FLOWERS DIFFERENT
TYPES OF NUTS ARE USED.

YOU WILL NEED
small hay collar (see page 151)
terracotta pot
moss
selection of nuts
candle
glue or glue gun

1

Fix the hay collar to the top of a terracotta pot (the more worn the better, for
this project) using a glue gun. Then add
the moss with glue.

2

Glue a selection of nuts into position.
Here, an equal combination of walnuts,
brazil nuts and hazelnuts (filberts) have
been used.

CAUTION — Do not leave burning candles unattended.

SEASHELL POT

OFTEN DRIED MATERIALS DO NOT SUIT THE STEAMY ATMOSPHERE OF A BATHROOM OR SHOWER ROOM, BUT THIS IS A NATURAL DISPLAY THAT WILL BE VERY HAPPY IN THESE LOCATIONS. SEASHELLS CAN BE COLLECTED ALONG THE SEASHORE OR PURCHASED FROM SPECIALITY SHOPS.

YOU WILL NEED
small terracotta pot
reindeer moss
hay collar (see page 151)
seashells
candle
glue or glue gun

ABOVE
As an alternative to using nuts only on a winter candle pot (see opposite), experiment by adding small bundles of twigs (wired into place) as well as open fir cones. Check that the moss is pushed down away from the candle, so that there is no danger of it catching alight. If you prefer, you could use a larger pot and 2–3 candles. However, take care not to place the pot in a draught or the candles might burn at uneven rates or the flame from one candle might even accidentally melt one of the other candles.

CAUTION — Do not leave burning candles unattended.

LEFT
For best results, choose a candle that is in proportion to the pot and hold it well in place with plenty of damp moss pushed all around it. To help to keep the nuts dust-free, glaze them with a florist's clear sealer.

1

Take a good quantity of moss and place it in the base of the pot. Press it down firmly so that the pot is about half full. This will form a base for the candle to sit on, and allow most of the candle to be exposed. Next, glue the hay collar into place so that it fits inside the rim of the pot as near to the top as possible. Cover the rim of the pot and the hay collar with moss, gluing into place.

ABOVE
Candle pots decorated with seashells are relatively inexpensive to make (especially if you already have a collection of shells); they will also last almost for ever and conjure up welcome reminders of the seaside. To help keep the surface of the shells dust-free, spray them with a florist's clear sealer or apply a coat of polyurethane varnish.

2

Now you are ready to start adding the seashells. Make sure throughout this process that you leave a large enough space to take the candle. Build up a broad collar, using the larger shells to create the first layer and main shape. When this is complete, fill in all the gaps with smaller shells to build up an even appearance. Finally, add a small quantity of moss to complete the effect.

GRAND MIXED SUMMER POT

THIS FLAMBOYANT LARGE FILLED POT CAN BE CREATED WITH MANY DIFFERENT EFFECTS DEPENDING ON THE MATERIALS USED. IT ALWAYS LOOKS ITS BEST WHEN CRAMMED WITH A MIXTURE OF SUMMER FLOWERS, HERBS AND FOLIAGE. WHEN PLANNING THE COLOUR SCHEME FOR A DISPLAY, WORK OUT IN ADVANCE WHERE YOU ARE GOING TO PUT THE FINISHED POT AND CHOOSE YOUR FLOWERS AND FOLIAGE TO COMPLEMENT THE ENVIRONMENT ACCORDINGLY.

YOU WILL NEED
large terracotta pot
dry foam block
stub (floral) wires
flowers and foliage of your choice
knife
cutters

LEFT
Sometimes even the grandest of displays can be achieved with only a few ingredients: keeping the number of elements to a minimum simplifies the design work involved, but does not detract from the overall effect. Here, blue larkspur provides a wonderful rich contrast with the nearby tangerines, whose colour is reflected in the orange carthamus. The only other ingredient in this display is nigella orientalis, which has been used to fill gaps with its green spikes.

1

Trim the foam so that it fits tightly into the pot (see page 13). Make sure that you fill the pot completely, and that the foam is level with the rim. Cut a second piece of foam about half the height of the pot and with a diameter slightly smaller. Fix to the foam in the filled pot with stub (floral) wires bent into U-shapes and pushed through to the lower piece of foam. (You could of course try to carve this double-layer foam from one piece, but it is extremely difficult to achieve.)

2

Trim the bunches of flowers, cutting each variety to a length of about 4in (10cm). Do not discard the waste stems at this stage — they may be useful later to fill spaces, and to add a different texture to the finished display. (All you need to do is to wire them into small bunches and insert them into the display as required.) Wire the bunches (see page 150), either in single varieties or as mixed bunches. Remember to wire enough bunches — you always need more than you think.

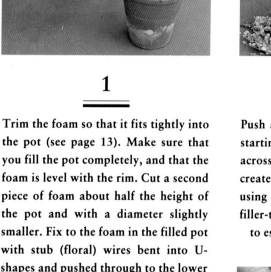

3

Push a bunch at a time into the foam, starting at the recessed rim and working across the top to the other side. This will create the large domed effect. If you are using bunches of one variety, place the filler-type materials into the foam first to establish the background colour.

4

Keep the large-headed flowers, such as roses and peonies, until the end. Turn your work regularly to ensure that you have not left any gaps and that the balance and mix are correct. Stand back from the display to check that it is the right shape and that the mix looks good. When you have added all the flowers, if there are still gaps, fill them with some of the trimmed stems.

RIGHT
It's surprising how putting just two flowers together can often create a successful arrangement. This simple variation on the Grand Mixed Summer Pot combines only two colours — yellow and pink — by using two varieties: solidago and miniature roses. Some of the roses were dried while still in bud, so this adds a little more greenery to the colour scheme than if only open rose blooms had been used.

ABOVE
Individual flowers are sometimes misleadingly delicate. Remember always to check the balance of the display as you work to make sure that the top is not becoming too heavy for the base. Here only four ingredients have been used: achillea ptarmica (The Pearl), white larkspur, lavender and peach roses. The finished display looks too big for its base but this can easily be remedied by placing the pot inside a larger container.

ABOVE

Whichever type of display you choose to create, and whatever your level of skill, the result will largely depend on the quality and type of materials available. In this variation on the Grand Mixed Summer Pot (see pages 31–32), a delightful range of flowers have been used combining different sizes, colours and textures: amaranthus (dyed red), eucalyptus, marjoram, oregano, peonies, poppy heads, nigella and moss. This arrangement has been given a special vote of approval — it occupies pride of place on the author's desk as it's one of his favourites.

LEFT
Whereas most of the projects in this book use dried ingredients only, this blue pine pot combines fresh and dry materials. Working with fresh twigs and flowers is much easier because they are pliable and less likely to snap when handled (most materials tend to become brittle when dried). Create the base of fresh pine branches first — you do not have to conform to a specific shape, it depends on what looks best. Then add whatever dried materials you have to hand. Suitable ingredients might include: fir cones, hydrangeas, lavender, red roses, lichen-covered twigs, sweet chestnuts (or any nuts) and moss (to fill any gaps).

RIGHT
Instead of opting for a single bunch of deep red or strong yellow roses, which would contrast well with blue and white china, this arrangement incorporates a range of pretty pastel shades which create a pleasing display. The small-headed fillers were added first, followed by the larger blooms which are more easily damaged. Eight different types of flower were used: alchemilla ptarmica (The Pearl), blue larkspur, lavender, nigella orientalis, oregano, peonies, solidago and roses.

LEFT
Occasionally a finished pot looks a little lost when displayed on its own and yet looks quite at home when placed next to another arrangement. These two variations on the Grand Mixed Summer Pot (see pages 31–32) share one ingredient which links them together. The pot on the left includes alchemilla mollis, bupleurum and solidago, while its neighbour also contains alchemilla mollis, along with marjoram, oregano and peach roses.

PYRAMID FIR CONE POT

THIS UNUSUAL POT DISPLAY IS A CONE SHAPE BUILT UP WITH FIR CONES AND MOSS. IF YOU FEEL UNSURE ABOUT BUILDING UP THE CONE SHAPE WITHOUT ANY FORM TO WORK ON, THEN CUT A SMALL FOAM PYRAMID TO GO INTO THE CENTRE OF THE POT AS A BASIS FOR THE FINISHED SHAPE. THIS DISPLAY CAN BE MADE WITHOUT USING GLUE, BY WIRING THE CONES AND MOSS, BUT IT IS QUITE HARD WORK AND ALSO MAKES THE DISPLAY LESS STABLE. WHEN EACH CONE IS WIRED, SIMPLY PUSH THE WIRES INTO THE FOAM AND BUILD THE PYRAMID FROM THE BOTTOM UPWARDS. IT IS EASIEST TO GLUE MOSS TO FILL ANY SMALL GAPS BETWEEN THE CONES WHEN YOU ARE COMPLETING THE DISPLAY.

YOU WILL NEED
terracotta pot
dry foam block
moss
fir cones
knife
glue or glue gun

LEFT
These woodland display pots make perfect winter and Christmas decorations. You could also spray or hand-paint a display in a variety of colours for the festive season — perhaps in gold, red or silver. Lightly spraying with white paint gives a delicate frosted effect.

1

Fill the terracotta pot with foam to produce a nice tight fit (see page 13). Make sure that the exposed top is flat, as this is the base for the pyramid of cones. Start by gluing a layer of moss around the top edge of the pot.

2

Next, begin to glue on the fir cones. Add the first circle around the rim of the pot, then when this is complete, add the next, laying the cones in slightly overlapping concentric circles so that you begin to make a pyramid. Glue the cones on horizontally, so that they point outwards. Keep adding more cones in circles and building upwards until the shape is complete.

BASKETS OF PLENTY

ALMOST ANY TYPE OF DISPLAY CAN BE CREATED IN THE
HUMBLE BASKET — THE RANGE IS ENORMOUS: RUSTIC
ONE-LAYER TRAYS OF HERBS AND GRASSES; GRAND TIERED
STRUCTURES; BASKETS BRIMMING WITH NATURAL
INGREDIENTS, COVERED WITH MOSS AND TWIGS, OR
EDGED WITH CONES AND SHELLS.

BASKETS OF PLENTY

The choice of baskets available is so varied that it should be possible to find exactly the right shape, size and colour to suit your intended project. Many baskets are inexpensive, but old or battered baskets can also sometimes be given a new lease of life, their distressed appearance actually enhancing the display. Even very poor quality, seemingly

PREVIOUS PAGE

This French flag flat tray basket is filled with regimented stripes of blue lavender, white achillea ptarmica (The Pearl) and red roses, all wired into bunches and inserted into foam so that they are level in height.

unattractive baskets can be covered with moss to create a useful container.

Although specific types of baskets have been featured on the following pages, you can, of course, substitute your own containers if they are similar or else adapt the design to suit the basket — whichever is the easier option. Alternatively, you can make your own hay and raffia basket (see opposite).

As with all the projects in this book, you should try to follow a few basic rules to ensure good results. Always remember to secure the dry foam firmly into the basket; if necessary, weight the bottom of the basket on the inside with setting clay before putting in the foam. This will ensure that even if the basket base is a little small a large arrangement will not topple over.

Sometimes the base of the basket will be uneven. To cure this, cut away any protruding pieces of cane or whatever,

but take care not to prune it so much that the basket will collapse. If the shape is correct for your chosen display but the basket has a handle that is not required, do not be afraid to remove it. Handles can usually be cut off neatly without leaving any trace of their existence.

Whatever design you decide to make remember to work carefully with your materials. Trim off any waste material and keep it away from the work area. Always try to think about the visual relationship between the various ingredients being used as you build up your display. It is easy to keep adding items with great enthusiasm, losing control in the process. Simplicity is often the key to a desired effect. Keep standing back to assess your work, to check that the colour mix looks right and that the ingredients are balanced.

FILLING A BASKET WITH DRY FOAM

1

Place a block of dry foam next to the chosen basket, and cut it to the same length and width. If the basket is large or an unusual shape, you may need 2 blocks of foam.

2

Trim the corners with a sharp knife, following the basic outline of the basket and making a more rounded shape, as necessary.

3

Press the foam firmly into the basket. Whether you trim the top level with a sharp knife or leave it standing proud will depend on the type of arrangement you are planning. Keep any good-sized offcuts for use in other displays (making a moss ball, for instance).

MAKING A HAY AND RAFFIA BASKET

1

Make a length of hay rope (see page 151), about 1in (2.5cm) in diameter, tying with raffia as needed. Coil the hay rope to form the base of the basket, using a glue gun to hold it together in a catherine-wheel shape.

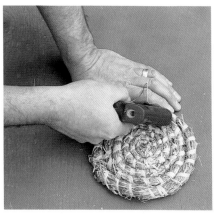

2

When you have made the base to the required size, cut the end of the hay rope and glue it firmly in place. Now make a second hay rope and glue the end to the base.

3

Coil the rope up into a cylinder, the same diameter as the base, gluing as you build. If you find this difficult, put something cylindrical onto the base to coil around as a guide. When the required height is reached, taper the end of the hay rope and glue into place.

MOSSING A BASKET

1

If the basket has a handle, add moss to this first. Tie one end of reel (spool) wire to the base of one side of the handle. Then gradually wind with wire round the handle, securing generous handfuls of moss underneath the wire.

2

Follow the same method with the sides of the basket. Tie one end of the reel (spool) wire to the bottom of the basket — you may be able to thread it through the weave, depending on the basket type. Then run the wire round the basket in an upward direction. Hold good amounts of moss firmly in place with the wire as you go.

Pack the moss tightly; be warned that the first time you cover a basket in this way, you will need much more moss than you probably expect. Leave any twigs, acorn cups and so on that are enmeshed in the moss where they are, forming an integral part of the natural look. Take care not to leave the mossed basket exposed to strong sunlight for any length of time (even just an hour a day) or it will fade very quickly.

FOREST CANDLE POT BASKET

THIS DRAMATIC YET FUNCTIONAL STRUCTURE IS MADE FROM A DOUBLE-RING BASKET BASE, WITH HANGING TERRACOTTA POTS ATTACHED TO THE OUTSIDE. THESE FORM NATURAL CANDLEHOLDERS, HELD SAFELY TO THE BASKET SIDES WITH A TIGHT BAND OF RAFFIA. IT IS MOST IMPORTANT THAT THE POTS ARE TIED FIRMLY IN PLACE AS THEY WILL EVENTUALLY CONTAIN BURNING CANDLES. THIS DISPLAY IS CREATED ENTIRELY WITH AUTUMNAL PRODUCE — FIR CONES, NUTS, TWIGS AND OTHER WOODY ITEMS. USE ANYTHING THAT IS AVAILABLE.

LEFT
Burning candles produce a wonderful glow in this autumnal display, which would make a sumptuous festive centrepiece for a dinner table or sideboard. Fill the centre with pot pourri, perhaps, to add an inviting scent to the overall effect. Although it seems elaborate, the Forest Candle Pot Basket is not difficult to make, uses basic materials and will last for a long time — it will only need an occasional dusting to keep it looking good.
CAUTION — Do not leave burning candles unattended.

YOU WILL NEED
good-sized round twisted vine basket (or similar)
hay collar (see page 151) (optional)
5 small terracotta pots
stub (floral) wires
bunch of twigs
fir cones
selection of nuts such as walnuts, hazelnuts (filberts), brazil nuts
moss
5 candles
raffia
florist's clear sealer (optional)
glue or glue gun
cutters

1

If you cannot obtain a basket with a broad top to work on like the one shown here, make a hay collar instead (see page 151) and glue this into place on top of a round basket. Make sure that the collar is level with the top, and is fixed to the inside of the basket. The collar needs to be about 1½–2in (4–5cm) wide for you to work comfortably.

Tie the terracotta pots one at a time to the basket, making sure that they are evenly spaced. Fix each in place by passing a strong stub (floral) wire through the hole in the base of the pot and through the top and bottom of the basket, twisting the two ends together.

2

Begin to add the decorative material to the basket. First, wire the twigs into small bunches (see page 150); then glue the wire to the basket.

3

Divide the cones, nuts and any other ingredients into five equal amounts. Working in sections, glue the cones into position on the basket. Do the same with the nuts and twigs until you have created a good composition that looks overflowing. Fill any small gaps with moss or small woody items. ▶

4

To keep the candles firmly in the pots, push moss down firmly all around the base of each candle until you have filled the pot to the top. Repeat the decorating process, turning the basket as you work, until you have completed the display.

5

Circle the whole display with raffia tied in a bow to finish. This also helps to ensure the pots are held firmly in place. If you wish to give the display a glaze, spray it with a florist's clear sealer.

ABOVE

Bring spring into your home at the end of winter by transforming the Forest Candle Pot with fresh daffodils planted in terracotta pots. Here, dried pomegranates, lotus pods, protea, fir cones, reindeer moss and twigs were used to decorate the basket, providing an excellent contrast to the green and yellow of the flowers. Cover the earth in the pots with fresh moss so that they blend well with the display.

RIGHT

The Forest Candle Pot Basket design can be adapted easily to fit other shapes, as with this handled version. The terracotta pots have been omitted here, and the ingredients varied to include mintola pods, protea, fir cones, a selection of twigs, and reindeer and sphagnum moss. The whole makes a delightfully unusual container for winter fruits; a small raffia bow completes the decoration.

WOODLAND TWIG BASKET

THIS IS A STRONG AND STRIKING ARRANGEMENT IN WHICH THE STARKNESS OF WINTER TWIGS IS OFFSET BY RICH RED ROSES AROUND THE BASE. IT IS PARTICULARLY EFFECTIVE PLACED ON A WINDOW SILL, SO THAT THE LIGHT CAN STREAM IN BEHIND AND THROUGH THE SILHOUETTED WOODY STEMS.

YOU WILL NEED
twin-eared basket
dry foam block to fit basket
twigs
moss
stub (floral) wires
mossing (floral) pins (optional)
red roses
knife
cutters

LEFT
*Roses always add drama —
particularly to a winter display. If you
feel that the straight line of roses is a
little harsh, you could soften the effect
by adding a few roses to the handles,
wiring the stems into the basket fabric.
To adapt this display for Christmas,
spray the twigs gold, and add a festive
fabric trim around the basket.*

RIGHT
*Use fresh moss in the display. In time
its bright green colour will fade but it
will last for longer if you keep it out of
direct sunlight. Try to arrange the
moss so that it falls over the edge of the
basket and is well pushed in among
the base of the twigs and the roses, so
that it looks as natural as possible.*

1

Cut the foam to fit the basket and push in firmly (see page 40). Push the twigs one at a time into the centre of the foam. Pack the stems together quite densely using as many twigs as possible to create a good shape. Place the taller twigs in the middle of the group.

Next, add clumps of moss all around the twigs to cover the foam base. Secure the moss in place with wire clips, made from stub (floral) wires bent into U-shapes, or use mossing (floral) pins.

2

Cut the rose stems to about 3in (7.5cm) and push them through the moss into the foam, to form an even circle around the base of the twigs.

A BASKET FOR ALL OCCASIONS

THIS IS ONE OF THE MOST VERSATILE OF
DESIGNS, AS IT CAN BE ADAPTED FOR
EVERY KIND OF NATURAL INGREDIENT,
TO ACHIEVE A WIDE RANGE OF DISPLAYS.
THE BASKET IS QUITE PRACTICAL, AND ITS
CENTRE CAN BE FILLED WITH ALL MANNER
OF ITEMS — POT POURRI, FRUIT,
FLOWERS, CANDLES — WHATEVER YOU
CHOOSE.

YOU WILL NEED
good-sized basket with handle
hay collar (see page 151)
stub (floral) wires
flowers such as achillea (Lilac Beauty),
achillea ptarmica (The Pearl), oregano
moss
cutters
glue or glue gun

LEFT
The finished basket, decorated with
soft-coloured oregano and filled with
garlic, is an appropriate arrangement
for the kitchen.

1

First, make the hay collar (see page 151) long enough to go around the inside edge of the basket. Fix it in place by pushing stub (floral) wires through the basket just under the collar; bend them up over the top, then twist the two ends together; repeat at regular intervals around the basket. The collar should be the same level as the top of the basket. Trim all the twisted ends of wire and bend them into the hay to hide them.

2

Cut the flower stems to about 3in (7.5cm). Wire together small bunches of flowers, either of the same variety or mixed (see page 150 for wiring). Attach the bunches to the basket one at a time,

gluing them into place on the hay collar. Work from the bottom of the collar to the top edge, making sure that you cover any visible wires. Try to keep a balance of colour and form, so that you do not end up with lots of the same variety close to one another. Check the display from different angles every so often to make sure that there are no spaces between bunches. Fill any gaps with tiny bunches of flowers, or individual flower heads, or alternatively use wired hanks of moss — always a reliable filler.

ALTERNATIVE METHOD

If you wish, you can create the same effect with a moss collar instead of one made of hay. Take a good handful of moss and form it into a sausage shape, about 1½in (4cm) in diameter, and long enough to go around the inside of the basket. Lightly bind reel (spool) wire around the moss, twisting round every ½in (1cm) or so up the length. Attach the moss to the basket with stub (floral) wires; then, add the wired bunches of flowers, pushing the wires down into the moss collar.

ABOVE

An overflowing pot pourri basket, filled with contrasting shapes and colours: pink roses and larkspur, blue echinops ritro, holly oak and achillea ptarmica (The Pearl) decorate a hay collar in mixed bunches.

RIGHT

This basket is decorated entirely with seashells and a little reindeer moss — a striking alternative to flowers. The method is just the same as that for the project given here, except that a variety of shells is glued directly onto the hay collar and built up in layers. For the matching seashell pots, see the project on page 29.

CAUTION — Do not leave burning candles unattended.

ABOVE

This basket is a pleasing summer country display that will last throughout the year. Here nigella, pink larkspur and roses are separated by bunches of alchemilla mollis and oregano. A rose-scented pot pourri in the centre of the basket makes the display twice as appealing and suitable for any room in the house.

LEFT

This basket makes a perfect Christmas container for wrapped mints and chocolates. The same technique has been used, but with a festive mix of nigella (which has been sprayed gold), amaranthus, red roses, poppy heads and bunches of cinnamon sticks tied with raffia. Add the roses at the very end of the arranging, as they are easily damaged.

WOODLAND HARVEST BASKET

FOR THIS FOREST-FILLED BASKET, TRY TO INCORPORATE ITEMS THAT YOU HAVE GLEANED YOURSELF FROM A COUNTRY WALK — LEAVES, SEED PODS, ACORNS, NUTS, MOSS, LICHENS — FOR A TRULY NATURAL DISPLAY. DO NOT WORRY IF THE MATERIAL IS A LITTLE DAMP, AS THE DISPLAY WILL SOON DRY OUT. FOR A LONG-LASTING PIECE OF WORK, YOU MAY WISH TO GLAZE THE FINISHED ARRANGEMENT WITH FLORIST'S CLEAR SEALER.

YOU WILL NEED
good-sized round basket
hay collar (see page 151)
stub (floral) wires
equal quantities of mixed nuts such as
walnuts, brazil nuts, hazelnuts (filberts)
fir cones
bunches of small twigs
moss
cutters
glue gun

LEFT
The finished Woodland Harvest Basket looks better the more haphazard and uneven it is. It can either be left empty, or you could add some simple flowers — wire miniature red roses into 2–3 small bunches, for instance, and place them in the centre of the basket. Or, as an alternative to flowers you could add a good woodland-mix pot pourri. If you have a fairly open-weave basket, make sure that you line the inside with a sheet of tissue paper first to prevent any pot pourri from falling through the gaps.

1

Make a hay collar (see page 151) about ¾in (2cm) in diameter and long enough to fit inside the top edge of the basket. Fix it in place with stub (floral) wires, each about 1in (2.5cm) apart: thread the wire through the basket, bring the two ends up and around the hay collar, twist them together as tightly as possible and tuck the loose ends into the collar. Using the glue gun, start adding the ingredients to the hay collar in small groups of each variety.

2

When you have added most of the items, wire up small bunches of twigs and glue into place. Cover with smaller nuts, and fill in any gaps with moss.

MOSS-EDGED BASKETS

ADDING A COLLAR OF MOSS AROUND THE
EDGE OF A BASKET IS A VERY EFFECTIVE
WAY OF PROVIDING A SECURE BASE FOR
MATERIALS.

YOU WILL NEED
handled basket
moss
reel (spool) wire
hay rope (see page 151)
stub (floral) wires

BELOW
*This moss-edged basket has been filled
with a mixture of plain deep green
and gold bay leaves to create a simple
but rich and glowing container
display. Some of the bay leaves were
rather dull and not looking their best,
so were sprayed with gold paint to give
them a new lease of life.*

RIGHT
This moss-edged basket is filled with pink larkspur (arranged loosely at random, though you could push wired bunches into foam) which complements the vibrant green sphagnum moss. The display works well with this rectangular basket but would look just as good in a more unusual shape.

2

Make a hay rope (see page 151) long enough to go around the top outside edge of the basket. Then cover the rope with moss, holding it in place by winding reel (spool) wire around it. Alternatively, make a sausage-shaped length of moss without using a hay rope. Bind the moss together, leaving gaps of about 1in (2.5cm) between each twist of reel (spool) wire. Keep the shape and thickness as even as possible.

1

Moss the handle of the basket first. Wrap plenty of good moss all around the handle, and twist fine reel (spool) wire around it to hold it in place. Start at the base of the handle at one side, working up and down to the other side. Take care to pack the moss generously under the wire.

3

Fix the moss length to the outside of the basket at the top: push stub (floral) wires at regular intervals through the basket and around the moss. Twist the two ends of each wire together and tuck into the moss out of sight.

LAVENDER AND ROSE BASKET

THIS FORMAL STRUCTURE MAKES GOOD
USE OF THREE POPULAR INGREDIENTS —
ROSES, LAVENDER AND MOSS — AND
DISPLAYS THEM TO THEIR BEST
ADVANTAGE IN CONCENTRIC RISING
PATTERNS. EVEN STALKS AND WASTE
LEAVES ARE INCORPORATED TO
DRAMATIC EFFECT. FOR THIS PROJECT,
THE BASKET WAS SPECIALLY CREATED
FROM TWO RINGS FIXED TOGETHER WITH
WIRE LENGTHS — BUT A STANDARD
SHALLOW ROUND BASKET WOULD WORK
JUST AS WELL.

YOU WILL NEED
round basket
dry foam block
moss
stub (floral) wires
lavender
red roses
knife
cutters

LEFT

*This staggered raised circle structure
is well suited to a number of different
ingredients — apricot roses and dried
grasses, for instance, could be just as
pleasing. When adding the central
roses, try to ensure that they are
placed at an attractive angle, facing
outwards, and that they retain as
much of their foliage as possible.
Ideally, when viewed from above,
none of the foam should be visible
through the flowers.*

1

Cut the dry foam to fit the basket (see
page 40) and push in firmly. Make sure
that the foam goes right to the edge and
to the top of the basket.

2

Fix hanks of moss to the edge of the
foam, so that it overlaps the top edge of
the basket. Use stub (floral) wires bent
double into U–shaped staples to secure
the moss in place.

3

Cut about 4–6in (10–16cm) off the
bottoms of the lavender stalks. Wire
them together at one end into even-sized
bunches, about 10 stalks per bunch (see
page 150). Press these in a circle into the
foam, just inside the moss.

4

Wire up bunches of whole lavender in
the same way, ensuring that they are of
even height and that the flowers are
level. Press carefully into the foam to
form an inner circle within the stalks,
leaving a central circular space ready for
the roses. Trim the roses and then wire
into bunches of 2–3 flowers and insert
into the centre.

PRESERVED LEAF AND FLOWER BASKET

DRIED FOLIAGE CAN FORM VIVID AND UNUSUAL DISPLAYS, ITS STRONG ABSTRACT SHAPES OFTEN LENDING THEMSELVES TO STRUCTURAL ARRANGEMENTS AS WELL AS COUNTERBALANCING THE MORE VIVID COLOURS AND SOFTER FORMS OF FLOWERS AND OTHER INGREDIENTS. LOOK AROUND YOUR GARDEN OR LOCAL WOOD FOR INSPIRATION. HERE, PRESERVED HOLLY OAK LEAVES (AVAILABLE FROM GOOD FLORISTS) IN AN OLIVE GREEN SHADE HAVE BEEN USED, BUT BEECH, MAPLE, FERNS AND MANY OTHERS WOULD BE JUST AS EFFECTIVE.

YOU WILL NEED
large basket
dry foam block
moss
stub (floral) wires
twigs
red roses
preserved leaves
mossing (floral) pins (optional)
knife
cutters

LEFT
Finish off the display with about a dozen strands of raffia tied into a bow. The mass of muted olive green holly oak leaves successfully provides a neutral background for the rich red roses.

1

Cut the dry foam to fit the basket (see page 40) and press firmly in. Make sure that the surface of the foam is just below or level with the top of the basket, to ensure that it will not be seen in the finished display. (If you like, you could at this stage cover the entire foam with moss — fixing it in place with stub (floral) wires — so that no gaps will be seen at all.) Start the arrangement at the centre, inserting the twigs first.

2

Trim the roses and the stems of the preserved leaves to the required length, remembering to allow enough depth to push into the foam. Steam the roses if you want to open the blooms a little (see page 150) and then push into the ▶

foam, either wired into small bunches of 2–3 flowers (see page 150) or one stem at a time. Start in the centre of the basket and work slowly outwards, keeping the arrangement balanced. Turn your work frequently as you go and check for any gaps. Be careful when adding the roses as it is very easy to break off their heads or the petals.

3

When you get to the edge of the basket, lean the flowers out slightly so that they almost look as if they are growing naturally. When all the flowers are in place, add moss to any small holes around the edge of the display, holding it with stub (floral) wires bent into U–shaped staples. If you prefer, you could use mossing (floral) pins but these can prove quite expensive, particularly if you need to use a fair number, and stub (floral) wires are extremely effective.

RIGHT

A subtle variation on the Preserved Leaf and Flower Basket can be created using preserved oak leaves, cream roses and sea moss. If you plan to incorporate twigs in a display, collect and arrange them while they are fresh and green because they become brittle and difficult to work with when dry.

ABOVE

*This basket is full of preserved brown
ferns, interspersed with large peachy
roses, thin twigs and sea moss. Ferns
and foliage that have been preserved
with a glycerine solution are available
from good florists. Ferns that are air-
dried (by hanging upside down) are
not suitable for display work as the
fronds become brittle and snap off
very easily.*

LEFT

*This basket arrangement of red roses
and preserved copper beech (dyed
green), surrounded by a base of
reindeer moss, was created in the
same way as the Preserved Leaf and
Flower Basket (page 61). The small
terracotta pot was simply filled with
foam, moss and single rose stems.*

GRAND MIXED GARDEN BASKET

THIS IS A BOLD, EXTRAVAGANT DISPLAY, SO USE THE BEST MATERIALS YOU CAN FIND. THE QUANTITY OF INGREDIENTS REQUIRED DEPENDS VERY MUCH ON THE SIZE OF BASKET, BUT THE IDEA IS TO CREATE A GRAND AND ABUNDANT MIXTURE, AS THE NAME SUGGESTS. TO ACHIEVE AN OVERFLOWING BASKET THAT APPEARS NATURAL AND SPONTANEOUS WITHOUT LOOKING CRAMMED OR MESSY REQUIRES CAREFUL PLANNING AND PLACING EACH ITEM WITH CONSIDERABLE THOUGHT.

YOU WILL NEED
large round or oval basket
dry foam block (you may need 2)
stub (floral) wires
8–10 bunches of flowers including
alchemilla mollis, hydrangeas,
lavender, marjoram, nigella, peonies,
pink roses
knife
cutters

LEFT
Peonies, roses, lavender and hydrangea flower heads have been used in this sumptuous basket display. To ensure that the flowers retain their colours for as long as possible, keep the display out of direct sunlight, perhaps giving it pride of place in the centre of the room.

1

Cut the foam to fit the basket (see page 40) and press in firmly. Make sure that the top of the foam is level. Then place a second piece of foam on top of the first — it should be about two-thirds the size of the base piece. Fix firmly in place with 3–4 U–shaped staples made by bending stub (floral) wires in half.

2

Separate all the flowers and make a pile of each variety. Trim the stems so that they are all about 4in (10cm) long. Form the smaller flowers into bunches about 2–3in (5–7.5cm) wide — leave larger flowers on their own — and wire (see page 150). Leave at least 2in (5cm) of stub (floral) wire hanging at the base of the stems and push into the foam. ▶

Don't work in one place, but add the bunches in an S–shape through the display, working from one side to the other as you build up the layers.

3

Build up the display, creating the background colour first with all the filler-type materials. Save the larger peonies, roses and so on until last or you may damage them as you work. The aim is to create a well-filled dome. Try to arrange the flowers so that the colours flow into each other through the display. The design should be as fluid as possible

with no harsh lines between the different elements. Allow the flowers to hang well over the edge of the basket; to achieve this, work horizontally into the foam around the sides, as well as vertically.

RIGHT

This version of the Grand Mixed Garden Basket was created with achillea ptarmica (The Pearl), bay leaves, lavender, marjoram, mint, poppy heads and oregano — all of which combine to give a wonderful fresh perfume and a perfect arrangement for a dark kitchen corner.

BELOW

Alchemilla mollis, mint, yellow roses and solidago are combined here to give a variation in yellow and green on the Grand Mixed Garden Basket. Even though it is dried, the mint still gives off a powerful aroma; the small bunches of roses are deliberately kept well spaced which in fact draws more attention to them.

TRADITIONAL TIERED BASKET

THIS REGIMENTED FORMAL DESIGN CAN BE VERY EFFECTIVE AND IS ONE OF THE EASIEST FOR BEGINNERS TO PERFECT. SO LONG AS YOU MAKE SURE THAT EACH LAYER OF MATERIALS IS THE CORRECT HEIGHT, YOU SHOULD MAKE A DRAMATIC DISPLAY, THE LOOSE AND FLOWING INGREDIENTS COMBINING WELL WITHIN THE CONFINES OF A DISCIPLINED STRUCTURE.

YOU WILL NEED
rectangular basket
dry foam block
flowers and foliage of your choice such
as wheat, lavender, roses
moss
stub (floral) wires
mossing (floral) pins (optional)
knife
scissors or cutters

LEFT
This simple structured display is most effective when created as a flat-backed piece which can be placed against a wall or perhaps used to fill a fireplace during the summer months. It is also particularly well suited for window sills — the wheat will shield the flowers in front so they will last for longer before their colours fade.

1

Cut the dry foam block to fill the basket (see page 40) and press firmly in. Start in the centre of the foam with the tallest ingredient (wheat in this case), wired into bunches of 8–10 stems (see page 150). Pack the stems closely together to achieve a good density. Check that the height balances with the basket size.

2

Lavender (wired into small bunches of 5–6 stems) is pushed into the foam directly in front of the wheat. Arrange the stems so that the lavender flowers come to just below the heads of wheat. Make sure the flowers are all facing the same way to achieve a symmetry.

3

Add the roses next, positioning them in front of the row of lavender. It will probably be easiest to add the stems individually. Try to keep as much foliage as space will allow, but be prepared to cut away a fair amount from each stem. Place the roses at slightly varying heights so that each flower head is visible.

4

Complete the display by covering the foam at the base with generous handfuls of moss. Fix this in place with stub (floral) wires bent into U-shapes or with mossing (floral) pins, if you prefer. Remember that fresh moss shrinks a little when it dries, so allow it to over-hang the sides of the basket at this stage.

LEFT

Vibrant blue larkspur and bright yellow roses provide a cheerful variation on the structured display theme arranged in a round basket. Air-dried hydrangea heads — faded slightly but complementing the yellow and blue above — were used to fill the lower part of the display, with handfuls of fresh green moss left to hang over the basket edge.

ABOVE

This flat-backed display in a willow basket from China combines two traditional favourites — lavender and deep pink roses — with dried mint, which provides a delicious strong scent. Generous quantities of fresh sphagnum moss are pinned in place to cover the foam in the basket, while also creating an excellent colour contrast with the line of roses above.

TOPIARY DESIGNS

THESE MORE ADVANCED DISPLAYS ARE SO-NAMED
BECAUSE THE FINISHED RESULTS LOOK LIKE MINIATURE
TREES THAT HAVE BEEN TRIMMED INTO TOPIARY SHAPES.
THE DESIGNS INCLUDE SPHERICAL GLOBES ON TRUNKS,
MINI-PYRAMIDS AND TIERED OBELISKS, AND BALLS OF
FLOWERS AND FOLIAGE.

TOPIARY DESIGNS

Creating successful topiary designs is one of the most challenging and rewarding ways of arranging dried materials. Trees and hanging balls can assume an irresistible, tactile quality particularly when they are made from unusual flowers or foliage. Yet even simple items, handfuls of glistening oak leaves, for instance, can be transformed into an intriguing eye-catching topiary design that seems to demand attention. One of the most pleasing aspects of these designs is that they can be used to fill gaps, since they can be given a trunk or suspended from above. When space is at a premium, topiary designs make ideal alternatives to traditional displays that occupy flat surfaces.

Although topiary designs look impressive, once you have mastered a few basic techniques, many displays are quite simple to achieve. They can be shown to stunning effect in the home or office, frequently bringing a sense of balance and formality to the atmosphere. Arranged in pairs beside or above a fireplace or on a long cabinet against the wall, their height can be used to fill spaces, and trees can also be used to bring colour to dark corners that are otherwise difficult to decorate. Hanging designs can similarly be used when standing space is in short supply, particularly if they can be hung from a beam across the ceiling.

PREVIOUS PAGE
Trees of fir cones and moss (see pages 90–91 for how to make them) combine simple ingredients with classic topiary shapes. These designs will look good indoors or in the conservatory.

ABOVE
A piece of dry foam simply covered with moss is one of the easiest displays to make. For instance, you can achieve a very effective topiaried look by placing a good-sized mossy globe on a terracotta pot. To make the pyramid tree, cut a foam cone into thirds and fix these to two short lengths of trunk before you begin to add the moss.

Points to remember
● Keep the size and height of the finished tree in proportion to the pot.
● Avoid making the trunk too thin: a short, thick trunk is preferable to one that is long and thin, which is likely to look unbalanced.
● Even if you do not want to put the tree on display in a terracotta pot, it is a good idea to make the tree with a pot as a base; then conceal the pot (which could easily be plastic, in this instance) by placing it inside a china or glass container, depending on your choice.
● If using a clear glass container, fill the area around the pot with a fragrant pot pourri that complements the colours of

the display, as well as adding a welcome perfume.

It is perhaps more important with topiary designs than other projects to read through all the instructions carefully before you start. There are more stages in the creative process, so you will need to set aside enough time for each of the elements involved. The majority of these projects have two parts: the potted base must be made several hours before the rest of the display is built. To make a topiary design, you need to set the trunk of the tree and fix foam firmly to it (see page 76). If you prefer, among other alternatives you can also incorporate a preformed dry foam ball into the display. Alternatively, use the following method which involves making a moss ball.

MAKING A MOSS BALL

This is a cheaper alternative to buying ready-made spheres of foam (which you then cover with moss). It is particularly cost-effective if you need a large ball but naturally involves more work and takes time. You also need a fair amount of moss – at least enough to fill a shopping bag. If you are going to add flowers to the design, make sure that the moss has thoroughly dried out (do not store it in an enclosed space). Fresh moss contains thousands of tiny spores which will quickly ruin a display with damaging mould.

YOU WILL NEED
large gauge chicken wire
dry foam offcuts
dried moss
stub (floral) wires
fine gauge reel (spool) wire
wire cutters
pliers
scissors

1

Cut a square of large gauge chicken wire, about 10–15 per cent larger than you want the finished moss ball to be. Make a pile of dry foam in the middle of the wire. Bend the wire up to wrap around the foam and form a roughly round shape. Tuck in more foam pieces to fill any gaps.

2

Push pieces of moss into the gaps between the foam, through and behind the wire, so that the foam is hidden by moss as much as possible.

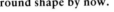

3

Gather the ends of the chicken wire together. (If you are going to add a trunk to the ball, leave a small hole at the bottom for the trunk to be pushed through.) The ball should have a fairly round shape by now.

4

Secure the loose ends of chicken wire with a strong stub (floral) wire, twisting it firmly in place with pliers. Cut off any excess pieces of chicken wire.

5

Tie the end of the reel (spool) wire to the mesh. Then pad out the ball with lots more moss to remove any holes or gaps. Keep winding the reel (spool) wire round to hold the moss in place. Finally, trim the ball with scissors, cutting off any straggly bits of moss to neaten.

ADDING FLOWERS TO A MOSS BALL

There is a simple art to decorating a moss ball. First, working at right angles to the surface of the sphere, push small wired bunches of flowers into the foam inside the moss. Depending on the type of flower, 3-4 stems in a bunch will give good covering power. Build up the basic pattern, adding bunches one at a time. Position every other bunch directly opposite the bunch previously placed on the other side of the sphere. Continue until you have added about 10–12 bunches. When you are satisfied with the height and spacing of the bunches, fill any gaps with moss.

FILLING A GAP WITH MOSS

Take a hank of moss about 3in (7.5cm) long and twist a short stub (floral) wire around the middle. Fold the moss in half and push the wire into the foam. The moss will open out and fill the area immediately surrounding the wire.

SETTING A TRUNK IN CLAY

The cleanest and easiest method is to use setting clay — good florists should be able to supply this as it is often used to weight displays. A messy but cheaper alternative is to use plaster of Paris (see page 77). Do not fill your favourite old terracotta pots with clay, because once it sets it is extremely difficult to remove. A better alternative is to use a cheap plastic pot, and then place it inside a terracotta pot or other container.

For the most realistic results, a branch from a tree makes an extremely effective trunk. However, a bunch of canes or straight twigs will do just as well. Gather a bundle to the required thickness and secure it at the top and bottom with stub (floral) wires. Twist the wires tightly so that the bundle is firmly held together. Finally, trim the top to a pointed shape so that it will be easy to push into the foam ball that forms the basis for the topiary. If required, spray the trunk with paint or wrap ribbon around it to match the colour scheme of the finished tree.

YOU WILL NEED
setting clay
terracotta or plastic pot
trunk (branch, twigs or canes)
dry foam ball or cone, or moss ball
reel (spool) wire
glue or glue gun
pliers

1

Push clay firmly down into the pot in all directions and check that it touches the pot on all sides. (Alternatively, if you are using a large pot — or simply to keep costs down — cut 2–3 wedges from the clay; stand the trunk in the pot and place the clay around the stem to support it well and hold it upright.)

2

Place the prepared trunk in the centre of the clay-filled pot and push it firmly, straight down through the clay, to touch the bottom of the pot. Leave the pot and trunk to dry. Depending on the temperature, the clay will set rock hard in 2–3 hours and turn a darker colour. The warmer the conditions, the faster it sets.

3

The clay contracts very slightly as it dries, so if you are planning on a heavy display, glue the base of the clay to the base of the pot as a precaution. Then fix the dry foam ball in place (or cone, depending on your design). Holding the trunk with one hand, push the ball onto it, so that it goes in at least halfway.

4

Tie the ball to the trunk with reel (spool) wire. Begin by fixing the wire to the trunk (twist it firmly in place, tying the end with the aid of pliers). Then take the wire up and over the ball repeatedly, as if marking it into segments (not too many or adding materials to the foam will be difficult). Glue or tie the end neatly to the trunk beneath the foam.

SETTING A TRUNK IN PLASTER

A less expensive option than using setting clay is to set the trunk in plaster of Paris. Although it can be messy to use, it has the advantage of a faster drying time than clay, so you may find it more convenient if you have little time to spare. Always clean plaster of Paris from tools or surfaces immediately after use, because it is extremely difficult to remove once it has set firm.

YOU WILL NEED
dry foam
terracotta or plastic pot
plaster of Paris
water, to mix
prepared trunk (see page 76)
reel (spool) wire
knife

1

Cut the dry foam into small, thin pieces and line the inside of the pot. This process is essential because when the plaster dries it will expand. The foam lining will ease the pressure, ensuring that the pot does not crack. Follow the instructions on the pack, and mix the plaster to a thick, creamy consistency. Pour the mixture into the pot until it is about two-thirds full. Take great care not to disturb the foam lining.

2

Push the prepared trunk into the plaster so that it reaches the base of the pot. Pour on more plaster until the level is about 1in (2.5cm) below the rim of the pot. The plaster will set quite quickly (in about 30 minutes depending on the size of the pot and your skill at working with the right consistency). Make sure that the trunk looks as if it is standing straight from all sides and hold it in place until the plaster has begun to set. When the plaster is dry (it will feel hard when you touch it) push a foam ball or cone (depending on your design) onto the trunk, and tie it firmly in place with reel (spool) wire.

MAKING A MOSS TREE

If possible, collect your own moss for this design: the colour should be vibrant and the mix of moss types varied. Moss bought from florists tends to be of uniform texture and shade, which can become a little dull. When collecting, pick up all small woody items, such as acorn cups, small twigs and fallen leaves, and try to find different moss varieties. Make a point of gathering moss from more than one place so that there is no danger of harming the habitat.

YOU WILL NEED
prepared trunk and base with foam
cone attached (see page 76 and above)
reel (spool) wire
assorted varieties of moss
stub (floral) wires
mossing (floral) pins (optional)
woody items including small
ingredients like cones, twigs and fungi
cutters
glue gun

Take reel (spool) wire and wind it a couple of times around the foam cone. Begin to add moss under the wire and slowly work around the shape, holding the moss in position with wire. The foam will quickly be covered. Alter the angle of the wire each time you go around the cone, so that moss is added in a different place each time.

When the ball is completely covered, cut the wire and tie the end to a stub (floral) wire bent in half. Push this into the mossy cone. Bend several more wires in half and go all over the shape adding more moss and securing it with wires or mossing (floral) pins wherever there are spaces. As the moss dries, it will contract slightly, so add generous amounts to allow for this.

Trim any loose moss that is hanging from the cone to create a good pyramid shape. Add any woody items (fungi alone were used here) to the surface with a stub (floral) wire or mossing (floral) pin. Alternatively, if you have a glue gun, simply glue in place.

Fill the base of the pot with handfuls of moss, adding more than you think you need to allow for shrinkage.

MAKING A ROSE TREE

WITHOUT DOUBT, ROSES ARE AMONG THE MOST EXTRAVAGANT OF FLOWERS. IN THE SAME WAY THAT THE POWERFUL SCENT OF AN OLD GARDEN ROSE CAN UNEXPECTEDLY HALT PASSERS-BY, SO DRIED ROSES CAN BE USED IN TOPIARY DESIGNS TO STUNNING EFFECT. COMBINE CONTRASTING COLOURS FOR DRAMATIC IMPACT, OR EXPERIMENT WITH MUTED PASTEL SHADES FOR A MORE SUBTLE LOOK.

YOU WILL NEED
prepared trunk and base with foam ball attached (see page 76)
10–12 bunches of roses
stub (floral) wires
small-headed filler flowers such as achillea (Lilac Beauty), achillea ptarmica (The Pearl), alchemilla mollis, bupleurum, marjoram, oregano, solidago
moss
cutters

LEFT
A tree of deep red and pale pink roses makes a delightful combination. The small rose pot in the background (see page 14) uses the same ingredients as the topiary design, so that the two displays sit perfectly beside each other. You could add a few drops of perfumed oil onto the moss, to give a strong rose scent to the arrangements. Never put oil directly onto dried flowers, or the petals will soften and may become mouldy.

WORKING WITH ROSES
You nearly always need more flowers to make a topiary design than you might at first imagine. Even a small tree will take 60–80 roses. To increase the size of the flower heads, steam them open a little (see page 150) before use. Many dried roses have a brown centre to the flower head, so when steaming make sure that the petals only open slightly so that any discoloured parts remain hidden.

1

Separate the bunches of roses and steam open any individual blooms as required (see page 150). Trim the stems about 3–4in (7.5–10cm) from the base of the flower head. This length will vary depending on the size you want the finished tree to be. If the stems are too long it becomes difficult to push the wired bunches into the foam ball and to reach down between the bunches as more material is added.

2

Wire small bunches of 3–4 flowers together, leaving the leaves attached to the stems wherever possible. You can also add to the greenery at this stage by trimming leaves from the waste stems and wiring the extra foliage to the flowers. Keep the wiring process as neat as possible and take care not to snap off any of the heads. To create a perfect round, the flowers must be wired so that they align at the same level.

3

Push the wired bunches one at a time into the foam ball. Work in turn on one side and then another, building a basic shape all around the sphere. When you have added 10–12 bunches and you are satisfied with the shape, start to fill the spaces in between with your chosen filler flower. Always support the foam ball with a hand on the opposite side to where you are working. Resist holding the trunk while you add material — this will only weaken the join between the foam and the trunk each time flowers are added.

4

When all the flowers are in place, there may still be gaps occurring at even intervals around the ball. Moss is excellent for filling small spaces, especially as its rich dark green provides an excellent background to enhance the colour of the flowers. Bunches of wired stems can also prove effective. Choose stems which still have leaves attached and push them into the foam, so that the stalks stand slightly proud of the roses. To finish the tree, cover the base of the trunk and the setting clay in the pot with generous handfuls of moss.

LEFT

As with many dried arrangements, after a while colours begin to fade so that the display no longer looks its best. This large rose tree had survived a couple of years, after a generous spraying of clear lacquer fixed any loose material in place. To prolong the life of a rose tree or similar arrangement, blow or brush any dust and cobwebs from the surface with a good strong hairdryer (on cold) and a ¼in (6mm) paintbrush, then spray the whole tree — including the pot — with a fine coating of white paint. This technique can be applied to most old displays that you do not want to part with. Keep the paint can moving while you spray so that the paint is distributed evenly. Of course, you do not have to choose white paint, but if you opt for gold, for instance, you will need to paint the display white first or the colour of the flowers will show through to dull the golden shine. Adding a few fir cones to the arrangement will also add to the overall wintry effect.

RIGHT

This delicate tree combines a pale pink rose, which frequently boasts a deep strong pink centre turning to a pale peach on the outside, with a small rose called 'Lilac Beauty'. In time, its petals fade to a rich cream colour. Oregano is interspersed among the petals. Keep these flowers away from direct sunlight and the display should last for 2–3 years.

LEFT

A wonderful range of dried materials can be used as variations on topiary designs. These magnificent grey poppy heads need no special treatment and should keep for many years. Resist the temptation to spray them with a clear lacquer as this will rob them of their grey/white bloom. Depending on their strength, you may have to support the poppy stems with wires wound around them before you add them to a moss ball (see pages 74–75).

RIGHT

Topiary designs made with woody materials like protea provide a dramatic alternative to the more everyday flower mix. They are also ideal for a first attempt at topiary because the material is so sturdy that it is quite difficult to make a mistake. Cover the foam ball with a good layer of moss to prevent any foam showing through from underneath the protea. This tree has the advantage of an extremely long life, and only needs dusting to keep it looking its best.

A BLUE PINE TREE

NO FOLIAGE IS QUITE AS LAVISH FOR DISPLAY WORK AS BLUE PINE (SPRUCE), WHICH GIVES OFF A WONDERFUL AROMA WHEN YOU CUT INTO THE BRANCHES. THIS DESIGN IS WELL SUITED FOR DISPLAY THROUGHOUT WINTER AND MAKES A WELCOMING DECORATIVE TREE. IF IT IS FOR CHRISTMAS, MAKE IT A WEEK OR SO BEFOREHAND. KEPT IN A WARM PLACE, IT WILL GRADUALLY DRY OUT AND CAN THEN BE TREATED LIKE ANY OTHER DRIED ARRANGEMENT.

YOU WILL NEED
prepared trunk and base with foam ball attached (see page 76)
blue pine
stub (floral) wires
moss (optional)
roses
fir cones
chestnuts
walnuts
cinnamon sticks
rosemary
raffia
cutters
pliers

LEFT
This rather grand blue pine (spruce) tree is made in exactly the same way as the smaller version shown in the steps but on a larger scale. The foliage will stay fresh for much longer if it is left to stand outside in a sheltered doorway, but the dried roses may suffer from any damp in the atmosphere. The finishing touch is a bunch of canes tied with a rich green and red fabric bow.

TECHNICAL TIP
Because of the nature of the material, the display needs to be quite large if it is to look well balanced. Choose or make a trunk that is at least 3in (7.5cm) in diameter to suit the proportions of the finished tree. Make the base well in advance so that the clay is completely dry before you start adding the fresh and dry ingredients.

1

Cut the pine into lengths of about 6in (15cm). Try to work so that you will not have to use pieces with visible cuts, while wasting as little as possible. Trim the greenery to expose about 1in (2.5cm) of bare woody stems which you can push into the foam. Alternatively, tie a short stub (floral) wire to each piece to give more strength to the display.
Create the shape by pushing as much pine into the foam ball as it will take. Support the top while you work and keep the balance by adding stems opposite each other. Take great care not to split the foam. Thinner stems will tend to droop as the display dries out, so use these on the lower half of the ball. Keep the shape as even as possible and in good proportion to the base.
If you have any gaps remaining but no more blue pine, wire moss into small handfuls (see page 75) and work around

the tree to fill any small spaces. Pay special attention to the underside so that a good round shape is retained.

2

Wire the roses into small bunches of 3–4 flowers (see page 150), leaving a good length on each stub (floral) wire. Add them to the tree at random, so that there is a good amount of pine between each rose bloom.

3

Wire the fir cones onto stub (floral) wires (see page 150) and add these next, making sure a good balance is kept. Keep turning the display and stand back occasionally to check that there is balance between the different elements. ▶

4

Continue by adding the nuts. The following is the easiest way to attach them to wire. Take a stub (floral) wire and hold it alongside a pencil with the point facing down. Leave about 1in (2.5cm) of the wire standing proud of the pencil. Curl this piece of wire around the pencil to make a small wire circle. Apply glue to the top of this and sit the chosen nut on it. With any items that seem heavy (walnuts for instance), if you apply a little glue to the end of the stub (floral) wire before pushing it into the foam, it will help to keep it in place.

An alternative method is to use a glue gun to stick cones and nuts directly onto the blue pine instead of using wires, but this can be fiddly. Also, once you glue an item in position you are committed to it, whereas with items that are wired, you can change your mind about where they should go in the display.

5

When all the other materials are in place, add the cinnamon sticks and rosemary bunches. These should be wired and tied with a raffia bow.

6

Finish by filling the pot with moss. Other finishing touches might include tying a bunch of rosemary with a raffia bow and fixing it to the moss. Or you could try scattering on a handful of nuts. The display will happily last a year or two but the blue pine will lose some of its colour. It can initially be revived with clear lacquer spray. When it is really looking past its best, either replace all the sad ingredients or give the whole display a frosting of white and gold spray paint.

SEASHELL
TREES

SEASHELL TOPIARIES WILL LAST FOR EVER
AND ONLY NEED OCCASIONAL DUSTING
TO KEEP THEM CLEAN. THEY MAKE
UNUSUAL DECORATIONS FOR A
BATHROOM, WHERE THE ATMOSPHERE IS
TOO DAMP FOR DISPLAYS WITH DRIED
MATERIALS.

LEFT

*The process for making this tree is
exactly the same as that for the
seashell cone tree overleaf, with a few
differences. Instead of the foam cone,
you need a prepared trunk and base
(see page 76). You may find it easier to
cover the foam ball with shells before
pushing it onto the trunk. This will
allow you to rotate the ball as you
work, so that the shells being added
can sit on top of the ball while the glue
dries. Otherwise you might find shells
with hot glue falling away from the
foam. However, if you decide to
decorate the ball first, remember to
leave a hole for the trunk. Once you
have pushed the decorated ball onto
the trunk, fill any gaps around the
base with more shells and moss.*

YOU WILL NEED
terracotta pot, the same diameter as
the cone
block of dry foam
dry foam cone
stub (floral) wires
reel (spool) wire
assorted seashells, graded into size
moss
knife
glue gun

1

Fill the terracotta pot with foam block
(see page 13), making sure that the top is
completely level. Apply a layer of glue
to the surface of the foam in the pot and
stick the foam cone onto it pressing
down firmly.
Bend 2 long stub (floral) wires in half to
form large staples and push these
through opposite sides of the cone and
down into the foam in the pot. Leave for
2–3 minutes while the glue dries.
Tie reel (spool) wire around the base of
the cone, then twist the wire round and
round the cone to the top. Repeat the
process from top to bottom, crisscrossing the first layer of wire. This will
create a good base to glue onto.

2

Beginning at the rim of the pot, start to
glue shells into place. Apply glue to each
shell and let it cool slightly before
adding to the foam. This will ensure
that the hot glue does not melt the cone
out of shape. Use the largest shells at the
bottom and choose gradually smaller
ones as you work upwards. As the shells
are added, push a little moss between
them to fill any holes but keep the moss
to a minimum or it may swamp the
shells and look too heavy. Try to mix
the type and colour of the shells as you
work. Also, remember to stand back
from time to time to check that the
overall balance is correct.

RIGHT
*Hoarders may already have a
collection of seashells from childhood
forays onto beaches, but if you are
collecting from scratch take care not
to break any conservation laws.
Similarly, if you are buying seashells,
make sure that your source is not
harmful to the environment.*

MAKING FIR CONE TREES

ONLY USE VERY DRY CONES FOR THESE
DISPLAYS BECAUSE FRESH, WET ONES
WILL OPEN UP AS THEY DRY OUT,
DISTORTING THE FINISHED SHAPE AS
THEY EXPAND. SIMILARLY, DO NOT KEEP
THE FINISHED TREE IN A DAMP PLACE
(OUTSIDE OR IN A BATHROOM, FOR
EXAMPLE), OR THE REVERSE WILL HAPPEN
AND YOU WILL NEED TO ADD MOSS TO
FILL THE GAPS CREATED AS THE CONES
CLOSE UP.

YOU WILL NEED
For the ball tree:
prepared trunk and base with foam ball
attached (see page 76)
fir cones
stub (floral) wires
moss
For the cone tree:
terracotta pot, the same diameter as
the foam cone
dry foam block
dry foam cone
3–4 short canes (optional)
stub (floral) wires
reel (spool) wire
moss
fir cones
glue gun (optional)
cutters
pliers

ABOVE
*Displays which are inexpensive to
create are always satisfying,
particularly as they can look just as
effective as more costly creations. You
should be able to find all the materials
for these trees in local woods or a
garden shed — only a little florists'
material is needed to complete this
unusual display. The most expensive
element is time: it is quite fiddly
working with cones so allow long
enough to complete the creation
without rushing. Spray the finished
trees with a little clear lacquer to give
them a fresh shine.*

1

If you do not have a glue gun, before you begin wire each fir cone by looping about 4in (10cm) of stub (floral) wire around the cone as close to the base as possible.

2

Secure the wire by twisting the end around the stem.

3

Add the wired fir cones to the tree by pushing them into the foam, working from the bottom upwards. Add hanks of moss firmly secured with stub (floral) wires (see page 75) to fill gaps as necessary.

If you are using a glue gun, you do not have to wire the fir cones but can stick them directly onto the foam. Apply the glue to each cone in turn and let it cool slightly so that the hot glue does not melt the foam. When the foam ball is completely covered, check that there are no small spaces in need of moss.

MAKING A TOPIARY CONE TREE

The process for making this tree is very similar to making the round cone tree (left). Fill the terracotta pot with the block of dry foam (see page 13), ensuring that the top is level. Cover the foam with a layer of glue and push the foam cone firmly onto it. (If you do not have a glue gun, push 3–4 short canes into the foam in the pot and then push the cone onto these, making sure that the cone is vertical and not at an angle.) Bend 2 long stub (floral) wires in half to form large staples and push these through opposite sides of the cone and down into the foam in the pot. This will ensure that the two foam halves do not come apart.

Tie reel (spool) wire firmly round the base of the cone and twist the wire round and round to the top. Then repeat the process in the reverse direction crisscrossing the first layer of wire. This creates a good gluing base. With this tree, fix moss in place with the wired cones as you add them to the display.

MAKING TOPIARY BALLS

IF YOU ARE SHORT OF STANDING SPACE FOR DISPLAYS, THESE MAKE A DELIGHTFUL ALTERNATIVE. THEY ARE CREATED WITH THE SAME TECHNIQUES AS THE ROUND TOP OF A TOPIARY DESIGN, ALTHOUGH THEY ARE A LITTLE MORE DIFFICULT TO MAKE BECAUSE THEY HAVE TO BE HANDLED WITH GREAT CARE, ENSURING THAT YOU DO NOT DAMAGE ANY OF THE MATERIALS AS YOU WORK. ROSES, IN PARTICULAR, ARE VERY BRITTLE AND FRAGILE.

IF YOU PREFER, YOU COULD BALANCE A FOAM BALL ON A STEM OR TRUNK WHILE YOU ADD MOST OF THE DECORATIVE MATERIALS, AND THEN YOU CAN FILL IN THE HOLE TO COMPLETE THE FLORAL DECORATION. THIS PROCEDURE WILL HELP YOU TO KEEP HANDLING THE DELICATE MATERIALS TO A MINIMUM.

YOU WILL NEED
foam ball
stub (floral) wires
assorted flower heads such as achillea (Lilac Beauty), ambrosinia, blue larkspur, marjoram, nigella orientalis, oregano, roses
ribbon

BELOW
Topiary balls can be successfully made with one single ingredient or with a combination of two or three. Ribbons complement the colour scheme.

1

Fix the hanging wire through the foam ball before you add any flowers. Bend a long stub (floral) wire in half like a large staple and push it through the ball.

2

Leave about 1in (2.5cm) of the looped wire sticking above the surface (this is what you will thread the ribbon through). Twist the 2 ends of the stub (floral) wire neatly together underneath the ball.

3

Wire together bunches of 3–4 flower heads (see page 150) and stems of foliage. Insert them in turn into the sphere, keeping the design as balanced as possible and turning the ball gently in your hands as you work. Choose complementary or contrasting colours, depending on your desired effect and on where you plan to hang the finished ball. Trim the completed balls with lavish ribbons finished with a bow.

BELOW

Roses look delightful when used in topiary balls, but take great care when handling the flowers as the petals tend to crumble easily. When you first start to work on a ball, cut all the stems to the same length before you begin, so that it will be easier for you to achieve a perfect round shape. As you work, trim the stems and adjust the flowers so that they are all at the same height.

DESIGNING WITH LEAVES

FOLIAGE IS OFTEN ONLY USED IN DISPLAYS AS A FILLER AND THE POSSIBILITIES FOR WORKING WITH IT AS A MATERIAL IN ITS OWN RIGHT ARE FREQUENTLY OVERLOOKED. YET, BY EXPERIMENTING WITH LEAVES, YOU CAN CREATE UNUSUAL DESIGNS WHICH HAVE GREAT IMPACT. COPPER BEECH AND OAK ARE THE MOST COMMON TYPES OF PRESERVED FOLIAGE, BUT FROM A GOOD SUPPLIER YOU SHOULD ALSO BE ABLE TO OBTAIN BOXWOOD, BUGHINA, EUCALYPTUS, HOYA, LEATHER LEAF FERN AND POPLAR, AMONG OTHERS.

Preserved materials are much easier to work with than foliage which has simply been left to dry naturally.

If the foliage is wrapped in plastic or polythene when you buy it, leave it to hang in a warm dry place for a few days to ensure that any residue preservative has time to evaporate. Be warned that if the material is dyed (which helps to bring out the colour of the plant), dye might drip from the stems of the hanging bunch.

Similarly, if the material is very dry, wrap it loosely in paper and hang it upside down in the kitchen. Every now and again, crumple a leaf to check whether its texture has improved.

LEFT

These unusual trees will add interest to a garden or conservatory at any time of year. While looking impressive, they are also among the simplest of topiary designs. Set a trunk in a plastic pot filled with clay or plaster of Paris (see pages 76–77) and fix a foam cone to the trunk. Wind reel (spool) wire 2–3 times around the pot to give a secure starting point, then continue to wind from the bottom upwards, holding moss firmly in place as you do so. Now cover the foam cone with small wired bunches of 6–8 preserved oak leaves. Push them in at random, allowing the leaves to fan out. Use smaller bunches of 2–3 leaves to fill any unwanted gaps. The result is a perfect mini–oak tree! Here a pair are displayed in stepped sequence beside a mossy ball, also one of the easiest sculpture designs to make (see pages 74–75 for method).

BELOW

These striking preserved oak leaf sculptures are extremely time-consuming to construct, but although the method is fiddly, it is quite straightforward. Whether using a foam cone or ball, pin each preserved oak leaf in place with a mossing (floral) pin, working from the top downwards. Then position the next leaf to hide the previous pin. Alternatively, fix the leaves in place with glue. The sculptures make an interesting, unexpected focal point and, if you have the patience to make two, make a cone to place beside a sphere for maximum impact.

These two small trees are a stunning pair, made using only limited materials. The green tree simply consists of preserved poplar leaves, which were pinned into a foam cone with mossing (floral) pins. Its companion was made with bughina leaves, pinned in place with a bundle of lavender and cinnamon sticks. The key to success is to overlap the leaves so that they hide the mossing (floral) pins. You might find it easier to use a glue gun as well as pins. The raffia bows look as though they are holding leaves in place, but in this instance they are purely decorative.

These windswept, almost haphazard preserved fern trees look deceptively simple but are quite difficult to make. However, the basics are straightforward: prepare each pot with a trunk in the normal way (see page 76) and cover the setting clay or plaster of Paris with moss to finish — if using clay, pin the moss in place immediately so that it is held firmly as the clay sets. Fix a dry foam cone or ball to each trunk with reel (spool) wire (see page 76). Then attach a rough layer of moss to the foam, using stub (floral) wires or mossing (floral) pins (see page 75) — this does not have to look perfect as most of the moss will be hidden, with only a little showing through the foliage. Wire the stems of the ferns (see page 150). Give the display as much movement as you can by adding the ferns at angles, so that they look as if they flow into each other. For once the aim is not a smooth-shaped topiary design, but you will still need to stand back and check the balance from all sides.

GARLANDS AND SWAGS

FROM GLORIOUS SWAGS OF MIXED FLOWERS TO MOSSY
GARLANDS DECORATED WITH TWIGS, CONES, PODS AND
FUNGI, THIS CHAPTER IS FILLED WITH INSPIRATIONAL
IDEAS AND SUGGESTIONS FOR WAYS TO EXPAND YOUR
REPERTOIRE, FROM SMALL DESIGNS TO MORE
AMBITIOUS PROJECTS.

GARLANDS AND SWAGS

Garlands and swags are frequently among the most impressive of displays, whether draped over a fireplace or portal, or hung as a grand welcome on a front door. From the simplest circle of hay and twigs to the most extravagant of swags, perhaps festooned with shells or surrounding burning candles in terracotta pots, their strong outlines and shapes have great visual impact.

There are grand and small-scale designs in this section to suit every occasion and situation. You might want to transform a dull part of the house or bare wall with an overflowing colourful flower and foliage circle; or create a seasonal swag for the fireplace at Christmas; or design sumptuous table centrepieces and miniature individual place swags for impressive dinner party styling.

Garlands and swags, in particular, are in many ways more complicated to produce than pot or basket displays, but the techniques are in fact quite straightforward and the results here quite achievable. It is the sheer size of many displays that makes them a challenge. Above all, you need plenty of space in which to work if you are to keep organized. First, make sure that your work surface is at the right height. It will also help if you wear comfortable shoes — the pieces are best made if you remain standing, especially as you should often move back to assess the work's progress, and you will probably need to be on your

PREVIOUS PAGE
Garlands can be successfully made with many different ingredients, but nuts, cones and dried grasses work particularly well, perhaps with a festive spray of metallic paint.

feet to select materials from the gathered piles. To make an average swag, it is best to have a work surface measuring about 6 × 6ft (1.8 × 1.8m). You can of course assemble a swag in less space, but it is not so easy.

A few guidelines:
● Always build a swag on a flat work surface, unless you are creating one which will be viewed from all angles and which would be best suspended from a hook, for instance, while you work.
● Build in a zigzag style backwards and forwards across your chosen base, making sure that the ingredients touch the work surface as you attach them. This is important so that there are no gaps down the side of the display.

MAKING A HAY RING

This basic hay ring forms the base for a whole range of different display pieces, not only garlands and wreaths. It can also be used as an attachment on baskets and other containers, providing a flat wide surface to which materials can be wired or glued. With only a few embellishments, it could even make an attractive display piece in its own right. For instance, you could spray it gold and add hydrangea heads and a few roses for a festive table centrepiece.

YOU WILL NEED
good-sized bundle of hay
reel (spool) wire
cutters
scissors

● Work along the length of a swag or around the circle of a garland, to maintain an attractive balance and flow to the work — it is very easy to lose concentration and build up too much of one material in just one area.
● If you are trying to create an even look, do not add large bunches of any one type of flower or foliage to a swag or garland. Try to add only two to three stems at a time.
● Stand back from your work frequently to check that the balance and mix are correct, and that you have not added too much of any one variety in one place.
● When adding material, pull tightly on the reel (spool) wire so that the stems are trapped and there is no risk of them falling out. Add large and delicate items

1

Make a sausage-shaped rope of hay, packing the hay as tightly as possible. Firmly tie the point where you start with reel (spool) wire, and then wind round and round up the length. Leave about ½in (1cm) between each loop of the wire. Keep adding hay as you work down the length. Every now and again, hold the two ends of the rope together to form a circle so that you can see how large the finished ring will be.

like roses towards completion of the display, particularly if you are fixing them with a glue gun. This reduces the risk of damage while working on the rest of the design. Also, you will be able to place them at a better angle, so that the heads can be seen well.

If you are creating a long, one-piece swag, ensure that you work from each end, meeting in the middle so that the flowers appear to flow from the centre. If necessary, you can always tidy the centre visually with a bow or trim.

A few of the designs incorporate fresh materials that will in time dry out. If you are using fresh and dry combined in a display, make sure that the fresh ingredients are not too wet and that the display is kept ventilated until it is dry.

2

To complete the ring, bend the rope into a circle, so that the two ends join. Bind them together and work back around the ring, adding more hay as required until you have an even, firm garland.

HAYING OR MOSSING A COPPER OR STEEL RING

A more expensive but easier way to make a hay ring suitable for garlands is to use a copper or steel ring as a base. This in fact consists of two rings (one is smaller and fits inside the other) which are bound together with hay padding. You can use moss instead of hay, if you prefer.

YOU WILL NEED
reel (spool) wire
copper or steel ring
good-sized bundle of hay or moss
cutters

1

Tie the reel (spool) wire to one of the copper or steel wires as a firm starting point. Take a good handful of hay and hold it between the two copper or steel rings to form a layer. Twist wire round the complete ring about every 1½in (4cm) to hold the hay firmly.

2

Add more hay and continue to wire it in place until the whole ring is covered. Take care not to add too much hay, or you will need more material to decorate the garland than is really necessary. Remember to keep a few strands of hay to one side and add them to the finished garland, if you want to give it a pleasing rustic feel.

3

If you prefer, you can make the ring with moss. This won't be as strong as hay, but is prettier — moss is a good choice if you want some of the ring to show through the flowers. Follow the same technique, wrapping the moss around tightly and securing with reel (spool) wire. Always use fresh moss.

ROSE AND POT POURRI GARLAND

THIS IS A DELICATE AND PRETTY GARLAND, WHICH USES A HOP VINE RING AS ITS BASE. THESE ARE FAIRLY INEXPENSIVE AND CAN BE PURCHASED READY-MADE FROM GOOD FLORISTS. IF YOU PREFER YOU COULD MAKE YOUR OWN, USING VINES OR TWIGS CUT WHEN GREEN SO THAT THEY ARE PLIABLE. WEAVE THEM TOGETHER TO FORM A RING AND LEAVE IT TO DRY COMPLETELY INTO SHAPE.

YOU WILL NEED
ready-made hop vine or twig ring
roses
moss
pot pourri
fir cones or woody material
cutters
glue or glue gun

LEFT
Although garlands are usually hung on a wall or door, they can be very effective as a table decoration, provided that they are not too large. Check that there are no pieces of wire sticking out from the back.

RIGHT
Try to keep the flowers and ingredients of this garland light and delicate. No decorative trimmings are really necessary, but you could perhaps add a rustic trailing raffia bow.

1

Steam the heads of the roses (see page 150) to improve their appearance if necessary. Cut off the stems of the roses and glue the heads to the ring, some in pairs and others as single roses. Try to achieve a good balance. Next, glue hanks of moss to the ring in the gaps between the roses.

Now apply generous quantities of glue directly onto the ring and sprinkle on handfuls of pot pourri to cover the glue completely. Finally, add the fir cones or woody items, gluing them onto the ring singly or in pairs. Keep checking that all the material is well spaced. Work on the garland in sections and move the base ring round as you finish decorating each part.

SUNFLOWER RING EXTRAVAGANZA

THIS FLAMBOYANT GARLAND CELEBRATES THE STRONG COLOUR AND ECHOES THE DRAMATIC CIRCULAR SHAPE OF SUNFLOWERS. IT IS CONSTRUCTED IN QUITE A STRAIGHTFORWARD WAY, BUT TO ACHIEVE A FLOWING FEEL OF UNRESTRAINED OPULENCE REQUIRES CAREFUL POSITIONING OF THE MATERIAL. ALWAYS TIE THE FLOWERS AS LOW DOWN THEIR STEMS AS POSSIBLE, TO AVOID A FLAT CRAMPED LOOK — YOU SHOULD ALWAYS BE ABLE TO PUSH YOUR FINGERS EASILY AROUND THE FLOWERS. IF POSSIBLE, LAY OUT YOUR PILES OF CUT FLOWERS IN A SEMICIRCLE SO THAT YOU DO NOT HAVE TO MOVE TOO MUCH EACH TIME YOU NEED MORE MATERIAL. IT IS IMPORTANT TO KEEP A GOOD BALANCE OF COLOUR AND SHAPE, SO STAND BACK AS OFTEN AS POSSIBLE AND TAKE A GOOD LOOK. IT IS ALL TOO EASY TO KEEP USING THE SAME PRODUCT TO COVER A PARTICULAR PART OF THE RING BECAUSE IT FITS; DO NOT BE TEMPTED TO DO THIS OR BEFORE YOU REALIZE IT YOU WILL END UP WITH A VERY UNBALANCED GARLAND.

1

Fix a stub (floral) wire to the finished hay ring, to create a loop by which to hang the finished garland. First bend the wire into a U-shape; then push it through the ring from the side which will become the back of the garland.

YOU WILL NEED
copper or steel ring covered with hay or moss (see page 101)
stub (floral) wires
selection of flowers such as alchemilla mollis, amaranthus, blue larkspur, carthamus, eucalyptus, nigella, sunflowers and twigs
reel (spool) wire
moss (optional)
cutters
glue gun (optional)

LEFT
The sunflowers in this garland simply generate sunshine; even though the flowers are dried it has an abundant, fresh feel that will inject life into any environment. It can of course be adapted for other seasons — with the addition of brown preserved oak leaves and more eucalyptus, for example, it could be quickly transformed into an autumnal display.

2

Check that the loop made by the wire is large enough, and pull or push the wire through the hay ring to adjust.

3

Twist the ends of the wire together and tuck them neatly into the hay. You may find it easier to add the wire loop after you have decorated the garland. This is because you may not know which way up to hang it and where you want the top of the garland to be (which is where the loop will go) until you have finished. You may only discover this by turning the garland round so that you can see it in all positions. If necessary, you can always add more than one loop and establish which way the garland looks best by trial and error.

4

Separate the flowers into bunches and trim each stem so that it is about 8in (20cm) long.

Start to add flowers to the ring. You do not need to wire them into bunches first; simply lay them in the position you want and wind reel (spool) wire round to hold the stems tightly to the ring. If you prefer, you could glue large-headed flowers into place at the end, but it is better to wire them in as you go along, if possible. However, if you do want to glue any, cut the stems short, apply glue to the end of the stem and push it into the ring so that the face of the flower is pointing outwards. Or, wire the stems (see page 150) and push through the ring from the front into the position required. Twist the wire behind into the back of the hay ring — this is how the sunflowers were fixed here.

Fill any spaces on the finished ring by gluing small bunches of flowers or hanks of moss into the gaps as required.

MAKING A ROMANTIC GARLAND

ONCE YOU HAVE MASTERED THE ART OF CREATING A BASIC HAY RING, ALL KINDS OF PRETTY GARLANDS CAN BE MADE. JUST VARY THE INGREDIENTS SO THAT THE OVERALL LOOK IS WELL BALANCED.

YOU WILL NEED
hay ring (see pages 100–101)
selection of materials such as achillea ptarmica (The Pearl), bay leaves, lavender, marjoram, mint, poppy heads and oregano
reel (spool) wire
cutters

Separate the flowers into bunches and cut the stems to equal lengths. Wire 4–6 stems at a time to the hay ring by wrapping reel (spool) wire round to hold them in place. Continue until you have filled the whole garland.

OPPOSITE
A garland made predominantly with sweet-smelling herbs will prove a welcome addition to any rustic wall.

BELOW
Flowers can help to make the mood for a special occasion. This delicate pale mix of ingredients looks very pretty in the centre of a table when all the candles are alight (take care not to leave them unattended). This design is made in exactly the same way as a garland for a wall, but a space is left for small terracotta pots which are fixed to the garland with stub (floral) wires. The candles are then added to the pots and held firmly in place with plenty of damp moss pushed around each candle to hold it upright.

CAUTION — Do not leave burning candles unattended.

BLUE PINE CHRISTMAS GARLAND

BLUE PINE OR SPRUCE IS ONE OF THE FEW MATERIALS USED FRESH IN THIS BOOK. IT RELEASES A GLORIOUS FRESH SCENT AS YOU WORK WITH IT, AND CREATES A MAGNIFICENT CHRISTMAS DECORATION. IN THIS DESIGN, RED ROSES AND AMARANTHUS ARE USED FOR A FAIRLY TRADITIONAL LOOK, BUT YOU COULD ADD APPLES OR TANGERINES FOR A LIVELY IF LESS LONG-LASTING ARRANGEMENT. PIERCE EACH FRUIT WITH A STUB (FLORAL) WIRE TO FIX IT IN PLACE.

1

Cover the copper or steel ring very roughly on both sides with hay or moss — this need not be thick but should be fairly even. Secure in place by winding reel (spool) wire round, leaving a space of about 2in (5cm) between each loop.

YOU WILL NEED
copper or steel ring
hay or moss
reel (spool) wire
blue pine (spruce)
amaranthus (dyed red)
stub (floral) wires
red roses
lavender
raffia
twigs
sweet chestnuts
fir cones
dried fungi
cutters

LEFT
This dramatic garland hung at the doorway provides a festive welcome for visitors. The complementary blue pine topiary tree was created with the same materials — blue pine (spruce), roses, lavender, amaranthus, nuts, fir cones, twigs and fungi — following the basic construction method on page 85.

2

Trim the blue pine (spruce) to lengths of about 6–8in (15–20cm). Take care not to spoil any branches by having cut ends showing on the 'best side' so that they would be visible on the finished garland. Divide the pine into four piles and begin to tie each stem to the ring with the reel (spool) wire. Use one pile for each quarter of the ring — this method of working will help to ensure that you do not use too much pine in any one place. Build up the branches on the ring, winding reel (spool) wire round to hold them in place and working from the inner edge to the outer in a zigzag fashion.

3

Trim the amaranthus stems to 8in (20cm) lengths, and wire into 4 small

bunches (see page 150). Do not trim — leave the wire hanging from each. Treat the roses in the same way, but cut them to a length of 4in (10cm). In each quarter of the ring, push a bunch of roses and a bunch of amaranthus, and tie the wires into the back of the ring. Do not leave any sharp ends.

4

Trim the lavender to 8in (20cm) and wire into 4 bunches. Keep a long length of wire hanging from each bunch, and wind a bow of raffia around the stems. Push each wire through the blue pine and tie onto the back of the ring.

5

Next wire up bunches of the twigs, nuts, cones, and fungi (see page 86 and 91)

and attach to the ring. Tie bows of raffia around the twig bunches as an additional decoration.

6

Add all these extra materials in small mixed groups, linking each group around the ring visually with one or two pieces of the same material. Be careful not to add too many of these items or they will spoil the overall effect — like painting a picture, it can sometimes be difficult to know when to stop. Finally, add a loop of stub (floral) wire to the back of the garland so that you can hang it (see page 105).

MAKING A NUT AND CONE GARLAND

THIS GARLAND CAN EITHER BE VERY SIMPLE AND QUICK TO MAKE, OR MUCH MORE LABORIOUS AND TIME CONSUMING, DEPENDING ON YOUR CHOICE OF TOOLS AND METHOD. IF YOU PLAN TO USE A GLUE GUN, IT IS VERY STRAIGHTFORWARD. HOWEVER, IF YOU ARE NOT GOING TO USE GLUE, MUCH MORE PREPARATION IS REQUIRED BECAUSE THE CONES AND NUTS MUST BE ATTACHED TO STUB (FLORAL) WIRES BEFORE YOU CAN BEGIN (SEE PAGES 86 AND 90). IF YOU PREFER, YOU CAN USE A HAND DRILL TO MAKE A HOLE THROUGH THE NUTS. PASS A WIRE THROUGH EACH NUT AND TWIST THE WIRE UNDERNEATH IT TO SECURE THE NUT IN PLACE.

YOU WILL NEED
ready-made vine garland or hay ring
(see pages 100–101)
fir cones
selection of nuts such as brazil nuts,
walnuts, hazelnuts (filberts)
stub (floral) wires
paper ribbon (to trim, see page 151)
glue or glue gun
cutters or pliers

LEFT
Once all the ingredients have been added to the garland, add any finishing touches. Here, a red paper bow has been lightly sprayed with gold paint and fixed to the garland with a stub (floral) wire.

1

If you are using a glue gun, simply add the various ingredients, beginning with the fir cones. Glue them to the ring in groups of 4–5, leaving a good space between each group. Stick larger cones to the bottom of the ring and use any smaller ones on the sides and the top.

2

Add the nuts after the cones. You can either add them in groups of one variety only or mix them together, depending on what you prefer. In either case, make sure that you fill the spaces between the cones to hide as much of the ring underneath as possible. Try to arrange all the ingredients so that they graduate from a thin layer at the top of the ring to a thicker one at the bottom.

If you are using wired nuts and cones, fix them to the hay ring by pushing the stub (floral) wires through the ring and bending them over at the back, tucking them into the hay.

LEFT
When a garland of nuts and cones is beginning to look a little tired, you can freshen it up with a coat of spray paint. Silver, gold and white provide the most successful frosting effect because some of the natural colour of the materials in the garland will show through from underneath the paint.
To fix a ribbon in place, either pass a stub (floral) wire through the back of the knot and thread the wire through the ring, or simply glue the bow in place.

MAKING A TRAY GARLAND

YOU COULD ALWAYS HANG A SMALL GARLAND LIKE THIS ON A WALL, BUT IT WAS DESIGNED AS A DECORATION FOR A ROUND TRAY, TO CHEER UP AN INVALID CONFINED TO BED. A GARLAND IS A SIMPLE, PRACTICAL ALTERNATIVE TO BALANCING A VASE ON THE TRAY IF YOU WANT TO BRIGHTEN UP THE PRESENTATION OF A MEAL WITH FLOWERS. IF YOU PREFER, YOU COULD MAKE HALF A GARLAND AND PLACE IT AROUND THE TOP OF THE TRAY.

YOU WILL NEED
copper or steel ring, or hay rope (see
page 151)
hay or moss (for ring)
reel (spool) wire
selection of flowers such as achillea
ptarmica (The Pearl), bupleurum,
hydrangea heads, marjoram, pink roses
cutters
glue or glue gun

1

If you are using a copper or steel ring, you need only one of the rings for this display (each ring consists of 2 wire circles). Wrap one of the circles of copper with hay or moss, tying it in place with reel (spool) wire. Leave gaps of about 1in (2.5cm) between each turn of the wire.

Alternatively, make a rope of hay (see page 151), again leaving gaps of about 1in (2.5cm) between each turn of the wire along the rope. Wind the rope around the edge of the tray every now and again, until you have achieved the required length.

LEFT

When making a mini-garland for a tray, use small-headed, filler-type flowers if you can so that you can keep the depth of the garland fairly low. If it becomes too built up, it might get in the way and make it difficult to eat off the tray. Using sprigs of lavender, or adding a few drops of perfumed oil, will add a pleasing fragrance to the finished garland.

2

Trim the stems of the various flowers leaving about 2in (5cm). Discard all the waste and lay out all the flowers so that they will be within easy reach when you work on the garland. Secure the reel (spool) wire to the hay or mossed ring and start to add the flowers. On such a small ring, it looks best if you work with a complete mix of different varieties all over the garland, so work up and down your line of materials to ensure a good, even covering.

Work from the inside to the outside of the ring, making sure that the flowers hang right down to touch the work surface, leaving no gaps. If you do find any small spaces at the end, add more material as required by gluing small bunches of flowers into place.

Note that it is often easier to add the roses right at the end. Cut the stems fairly short and then glue the flowers into position so that they are at the best possible angle. If you add roses as you go along, the stiffness of the stems can make them difficult to work with. If necessary, steam the roses open (see page 150) before you add them to the garland.

MAKING A SQUARE GARLAND

ALTHOUGH GARLANDS TEND TO BE ROUND IN SHAPE, A SQUARE FRAME CAN BE USED AS A SIMPLE AND EXCELLENT ALTERNATIVE. IF YOU DO NOT WANT TO KEEP THE DESIGN STRICTLY FORMAL, EXPERIMENT WITH DIFFERENT SHAPED STICKS — THEY DO NOT HAVE TO BE COMPLETELY STRAIGHT TO CREATE AN INTERESTING VARIATION.

YOU WILL NEED
strong canes or similar for the frame
stub (floral) wires
moss
reel (spool) wire
twigs
dried fungi
cones
pliers
cutters
glue or glue gun

LEFT
This garland, made with fresh moss, cones, twigs, fungi and seed pods, is the perfect way to brighten up an outside wall. It should last for a long time, though the moss will lose its bright green colour as it dries.

RIGHT
This triangular variation on the square garland is made in exactly the same way, and is also decorated with a simple mix of locally gathered woody items. The miniature terracotta pots are wired and glued into place. If you are going to hang the garland outside, spray the roses with florist's clear sealer so that they are protected.

1

If the canes are thin, wire 5–8 together to make one stronger length for each side of the frame. Use pliers to twist the wire around the ends of the canes. Then, make a square frame using the 4 cane bunches, tying them in each corner with a stub (floral) wire. Add a dab of glue to the wires to ensure that they are fixed firmly.

2

Cover the frame with moss, holding it in place with reel (spool) wire. Try to keep an even amount of moss on all sides of the frame and avoid leaving any gaps. Make the base secure, as this is what the remaining material will be attached to.

3

When the frame is completely covered with moss, tie the twigs onto it with reel (spool) wire. Add as many as you think look good, remembering what materials you have to come. If you do not plan to use a glue gun, fix the decorative ingredients to stub (floral) wires. Otherwise, start to glue the fungi and so on into position. Place the material in small groups. Hide any wires that show with extra moss.

MAKING GARLANDS WITH TWIGS

WHEN YOU FEEL CONFIDENT WORKING WITH DRIED MATERIALS, YOU CAN BEGIN TO EXPERIMENT WITH OTHER TYPES OF GARLAND. IT IS QUITE EASY TO CREATE A BASE USING TWIGS BUT BE SURE TO USE THEM WHEN THEY ARE FRESH AND GREEN (ONCE THEY START TO DRY THEY BECOME EXTREMELY BRITTLE AND MAY SNAP OFF IN YOUR HANDS). USE STUB (FLORAL) WIRES OR A GLUE GUN TO ATTACH FUNGI, CONES OR WHATEVER YOU PLAN TO USE AS DECORATION TO THE TWIGS.

LEFT

A simple, yet unusual garland can be created very quickly with a good bunch of willow twigs — though any type is suitable. Tie the twigs to a copper or steel ring, to give the garland a circular shape and firm outline. Fix the twigs with stub (floral) wires, then add whatever you like as decorations — dried cones, pomegranates and fungi, for instance. Here, the finishing touch is a green paper bow (see page 151) which brings a sense of balance to the garland.

RIGHT

All the materials in this garland were found in a forest; then they were separated into small bunches and wired into place on a copper or steel ring. The finished garland is particularly well suited to being hung outdoors. Twigs covered with mosses or lichens can give great depth to a display, providing an unexpected range of hues and textures.

MAKING A
MIXED SWAG

WHATEVER THE TIME OF YEAR, A SWAG
OF FLOWERS BRINGS A CHEERFUL BREATH
OF FRESH AIR TO THE SURROUNDINGS.
TAKE CARE NOT TO BE OVER-AMBITIOUS
WHEN YOU FIRST START MAKING SWAGS,
AS ALTHOUGH THEY LOOK DECEPTIVELY
SIMPLE TO MAKE, IT CAN BE DIFFICULT
TO GET THE BALANCE OF THE DESIGN
RIGHT. THEY ALSO REQUIRE LARGER
QUANTITIES OF MATERIALS THAN YOU
MIGHT EXPECT

YOU WILL NEED
hay rope (see page 151)
selection of flowers such as pink
larkspur, marjoram, nigella, oregano,
pink roses
reel (spool) wire
stub (floral) wires (optional)
raffia or fabric trim
glue or glue gun (optional)
cutters

LEFT
Take care when handling a finished
swag to ensure that nothing is
damaged while you move it to
wherever it is to be displayed. If you
need a very long swag, it is much
easier and safer to make short sections
and then cover the joins with ribbon
or fabric to give the impression of one
long continuous piece.

1

First, make the hay rope to the length you require (see page 151). Prepare all the bunches of flowers, separating them into piles so that you can see at a glance what you have available. Trim the stems of the flowers so that they are all about 7in (18cm) long. Discard all the waste and make as much room for yourself as possible. If you have enough space, arrange all the bunches in a semicircle within arm's reach.

2

Tie the reel (spool) wire to the beginning of the hay rope. Then bind on small bunches of each flower variety working in a zigzag fashion. Take the reel (spool) wire right round the hay rope and the flower stems. Tie the bun-

ches well down the stems so that there is air round the flower heads and they are not cramped. Check that each flower relates well to its neighbour and try to place the bunches so that the varieties seem to flow through the swag. Keep working until you have reached the end of the rope and can add no more material. Then bind the stems together and tie a knot in the reel (spool) wire. If there are any unwanted gaps in the swag, wire small bunches of a filler flower and glue them into the gaps or tie them in place with a stub (floral) wire. Complete the swag with a bow of raffia or fabric.

ABOVE RIGHT

Swags can be made with dried or fresh materials — or a combination of both. Here, fresh materials were used on their own to make a wonderfully sweet-smelling swag, tied with a gold and burgundy ribbon to match the surrounding decor. One of the main advantages of working with fresh ingredients is that there is less chance of the stems breaking or of flower heads snapping off. You might lose a few items as the swag slowly dries out, but if you select the ingredients carefully they should look good for many months to come. Choose any green foliage as the base, then add lavender, rosemary, fir cones and lichen-covered twigs for a simple yet effective design.

RIGHT
Although blue-and-white china makes an attractive display on its own, this simple swag of complementary blue larkspur, bupleurum and solidago draws the eye away from the basic white shelves, softening the hard lines and creating an unusual focal point in the kitchen. The impression of one long swag is misleading: two short swags have in fact been hooked onto the shelves behind and a yellow fabric ribbon used to hide the join in the middle at the top.

LEFT
A colourful swag draped above a bed makes a pleasant alternative to simply placing an arrangement on a dressing table in permanent anticipation of visitors. Here, a glorious mix of ingredients successfully creates a look of luxury: tied bunches of lavender (which keeps the room smelling fresh), pale pink roses, holly oak and nigella (both sprayed with a light layer of gold), together with poppy heads and fir cones. Everything was tied to the hay rope, in this instance using brown garden twine, though reel (spool) wire could have been used instead. The roses were wired (see page 150) before they were added to the swag, to minimize possible damage to the flower heads.

ORNAMENTAL DESIGNS

ONCE YOU FEEL CONFIDENT WORKING WITH POTS,
BASKETS, GARLANDS AND TOPIARIES, YOU CAN
EXPERIMENT WITH MORE COMPLICATED DESIGNS. FROM
UNUSUAL CANDLEHOLDERS TO AN EXTRAVAGANT TABLE
SETTING, THE FOLLOWING CREATIONS REVEAL THE
VERSATILITY OF WORKING WITH DRIED MATERIALS.

MAKING A CANDLE SACK

CANDLE SACKS CAN BE MADE USING JUST
ABOUT ANY MIX OF FLOWERS. WHENEVER
POSSIBLE, TRY TO CHOOSE MATERIAL FOR
THE BASE THAT WILL MATCH A
PARTICULAR SETTING AND ALSO
COMPLEMENT THE FLOWERS. REMEMBER
NEVER TO LEAVE BURNING CANDLES
UNATTENDED.

YOU WILL NEED
plastic bag
sand
dry foam block
fabric offcut about 18in (45cm) in
diameter
stub (floral) wires
reel (spool) wire
mossing (floral) pin (optional)
preserved ferns or leaves
flowers such as carthamus and
marjoram
candleholder
cream candle
knife
cutters
pliers
scissors

LEFT
*In this candle sack, preserved fern is
the predominant foliage, while
marjoram and deep red roses provide
contrasting colours.*

PREVIOUS PAGE
*This experimental design of woodland
materials spilling in all directions is
based on two dry foam blocks, bound
together with reel (spool) wire. The
moss is fixed with mossing (floral) pins
and all the other ingredients are wired
or glued firmly in place.*

1

Fill the plastic bag with sand to a depth of 1in (2.5cm) and a diameter of 5in (13cm) when the sand is patted down into a round. Tie a knot to close the bag, squeezing out all the air.
Cut a cylinder from the block of dry foam (this is much cheaper than buying one ready-made). Make it slightly smaller than the bag of sand. Place the sand bag on the piece of fabric, and the foam on top of the bag.

2

Gather the fabric up around the dry foam while also bringing the sand bag up a little around the base of the foam. Fix the fabric in place with stub (floral) wires bent into U-shapes, or by winding reel (spool) wire round the top.

3

Fix the reel (spool) wire to the fabric with a mossing (floral) pin or wind the wire 2–3 times round the neck of the base to make a firm starting point. Now add the preserved ferns or whatever foliage you are using, holding them in place by winding reel (spool) wire round the neck.

4

Trim the flowers so that the stalks are all about 6in (15cm) long and wire them into small mixed bunches (see page 150). Push the candleholder into the centre of the foam and start to add the wired bunches. Check that the flowers are at an angle leaning outwards away from the centre, so that there is no danger of the candle setting them alight.

5

Continue to add the wired bunches until the foam is completely covered. If any small gaps still remain, fill these with individual flowers or leaves.

ABOVE
This variation on the candle sack is made with pink roses, blue larkspur and mint, which gives off a delicious aroma.

CAUTION — Do not leave burning candles unattended.

PERFUMED BUNCHES

THESE DISPLAYS, REFLECTING THE FOUR
SEASONS OF THE YEAR, MAKE A
DELIGHTFUL ALTERNATIVE TO THE
UBIQUITOUS POT POURRI. THEY SHOULD
KEEP THEIR FRAGRANCE FOR MUCH
LONGER THAN ORDINARY PETAL MIXES,
AND ONCE THE AROMA BEGINS TO FADE
IT CAN QUICKLY BE RESTORED WITH
MORE DROPS OF PERFUMED OIL. IF THEY
ARE PLACED NEXT TO A SOURCE OF HEAT,
A RADIATOR FOR INSTANCE, THEY WILL
RELEASE MORE OF THE PERFUME. THE
METHOD IS THE SAME FOR EACH DISPLAY
BUT YOU NEED TO VARY THE DRIED
FLOWERS, DEPENDING ON WHICH
VERSION YOU ARE MAKING.

YOU WILL NEED
selection of dried flowers
long cinnamon sticks
stub (floral) wires
raffia or fabric trim
perfumed oil
moss (optional)
cutters

LEFT
*Only a few ingredients are required to
conjure up a feeling of spring in this
variation on the fragrant bundle,
which can be displayed in any part of
the house: alchemilla mollis,
cinnamon sticks, white larkspur,
lavender, oregano and yellow roses. A
few drops of perfumed oil added to the
finished bundle completes the display,
here complemented by pots of bright
yellow daffodils.*

1

Separate the flowers into bunches according to variety, so that they will be easy to work with. Take 4–5 long cinnamon sticks and place the first flowers so that their heads align with the sticks. Add the flowers so that there are flower heads at both ends of the sticks (opposite each other), with the stems meeting in the middle.

2

Build up the flowers so that there are flower heads running down the entire length of the cinnamon sticks from both ends and almost meeting at the centre. Tie the completed bundle around the middle with a stub (floral) wire. Cut away any excess wire and push the ends in among the stalks.

Tie a raffia or fabric bow around the middle and trim away any straggling stalks that are sticking out of the bundle. Then add a few drops of perfumed oil to the centre of the display. Alternatively, soak a piece of moss in the oil and tie it in place with a stub (floral) wire. This will release its perfume slowly and can easily be topped up when it has dried out.

ABOVE
This delightful combination, here displayed beside a clump of snowdrops, will bring an air of freshness to any room throughout the winter months: achillea ptarmica (The Pearl), cinnamon sticks, fir cones, lavender, oregano, poppy heads, deep red roses, stirlingia and lichen-covered twigs.

RIGHT

All you need to do is substitute a few of the ingredients to transform the display into a scented bundle that will brighten up the summer months. Here, achillea ptarmica (The Pearl), echinops, blue larkspur, nigella orientalis, pale pink roses and silene have all been added to the cinnamon sticks.

BELOW

This perfumed display captures warm rich colours that will cheer any dark corner through the months of autumn. These delightful ingredients complement each other: amaranthus (dyed red), carthamus, echinops, blue larkspur, nigella, solidago, yellow roses, fir cones and cinnamon sticks.

DECORATING A FRAME WITH SHELLS

THIS IS AN UNUSUAL WAY TO BRIGHTEN UP A BATHROOM, AND YOU COULD OF COURSE ADAPT THE TECHNIQUE FOR A PICTURE FRAME, RATHER THAN A MIRROR. MAKE SURE THAT YOU OBTAIN YOUR SHELLS FROM A RELIABLE SOURCE, OR USE THOSE THAT YOU FIND WASHED UP ON A BEACH, SO LONG AS YOU ARE NOT BREAKING ANY ENVIRONMENT LAWS BY TAKING THEM HOME WITH YOU. YOU WILL FIND THAT IT IS MUCH EASIER TO WORK ON A FRAME WITHOUT THE MIRROR IN PLACE. YOU SHOULD ALSO NOTE THAT A GLUE GUN REALLY IS AN ESSENTIAL TOOL FOR THIS PROJECT, OR IT WILL TAKE AN EXTREMELY LONG TIME TO COMPLETE. YOU COULD USE JUST A TUBE OF GLUE, BUT IT WILL NOT BE NEARLY AS EFFECTIVE. TAKE GREAT CARE WHEN WORKING WITH A GLUE GUN, BECAUSE THE GLUE IS HOT ENOUGH TO CAUSE AN UNPLEASANT BURN.

LEFT

The spectacular frame on this mirror requires endless patience and a board of seashells but it is well worth the effort. It might be wise to start on a smaller project, like the shell tree (see pages 87–88), so that you feel confident working with shells and a glue gun before you embark on anything quite as large as the mirror. You can ring the changes and fix any additional materials to the frame once it is complete. Here a twig bundle has been gently wedged (not glued) behind a few shells to create a slightly rustic look.

1

Check that the surface of the frame is clean and dry before you start. Begin in a corner and glue the first shells to the frame. Apply the glue to each shell before pressing it onto the frame. Try to choose shells that are in proportion to the frame and which sit well next to each other. The process is rather like building up a jigsaw puzzle and you might find that it takes time for you to feel in control of your creation. If you are not sure how you want the shells to look, arrange them around the edge of the frame and experiment by moving them from one position to another, before you glue any into place.

Remove any excess glue as you work because it is difficult to do so once it has set. Continue to work around the frame, adding shells as you go. They should almost flow into each other. Use smaller shells to fill the larger gaps and glue shells onto each other as well.

YOU WILL NEED
basic wooden frame
selection of shells
small terracotta pot
reindeer moss
glue gun

2

If you plan to add a small terracotta pot — perhaps to take flowers, fir cones or a candle — apply the glue to the side of the pot and stick it directly to the frame (not onto any shells). Build up shells so that they come right to the edge of the pot, and then glue smaller shells onto the pot itself, so that all the elements seem to blend together. If the frame is deep-sided, remember to add shells to the sides and not just to the front of the frame. When you have finished adding the shells, glue on moss to fill any gaps.

ABOVE

This starfish is not glued but instead is balanced in the small terracotta pot. From a distance, reflections in the mirror give a double-frame illusion.

MAKING A CANDLE RING

SMALL CANE RINGS CAN BE OBTAINED FROM GOOD FLORISTS, BUT IF YOU PREFER YOU COULD WORK WITH A LENGTH OF HAY ROPE INSTEAD (SEE PAGE 151), RATHER LIKE A MINI-GARLAND. ALTHOUGH ANY SMALL-HEADED FLOWER WOULD BE SUITABLE FOR THESE DECORATIONS, DRIED ROSES ARE THE PERFECT MATERIAL. IF NECESSARY, STEAM THE HEADS OPEN IN ADVANCE (SEE PAGE 150). ALTERNATIVELY, YOU COULD USE FIR CONES AND NUTS (PERHAPS SPRAYED WITH A FROSTING OF GOLD OR WHITE PAINT) TO MAKE CHRISTMAS CANDLE RINGS. IF YOU ARE PLANNING TO USE THE FINISHED DECORATIONS ON TALL CANDLESTICKS, MAKE SURE THAT YOU START THE FLOWERS WELL DOWN THE SIDES OF THE CANE OR HAY RING, OR THE BASE AND WORKINGS MAY BE VISIBLE AT EYE-LEVEL TO ANYONE SEATED NEARBY. ALWAYS REMEMBER NEVER TO LEAVE LIGHTED CANDLES UNATTENDED.

LEFT

If you are using more than one shade or variety of rose on a candle ring, glue them in pairs of different colours and try to position the heads so that they are facing outwards. Small leaves discarded with the unwanted rose stems can prove useful fillers, but take care that they will not be too tall and become a fire hazard. Never leave lighted candles unattended and always check regularly to see how fast the flames are burning, so that there is no danger of the rings catching alight.
CAUTION — Do not leave burning candles unattended.

YOU WILL NEED
small cane ring or hay ring (see page 100)
moss
selection of flowers such as roses and bupleurum
candle
glue gun
cutters

1

Glue a light covering of moss to the cane or hay ring. Try to make sure that no glue is visible (it turns opaque white when set).

2

Cut all the roses from their stems leaving as little stalk as possible, and begin to glue them into place. Position the ▶

roses so that you maintain a symmetry in design, unless you are deliberately aiming for a random look. Work on one side of the ring and then the other, to get the balance right.

3

After you have added the roses, begin to fill the spaces between them, using glue to fix whatever flowers or foliage you have selected. Make sure that the hole left in the middle will be large enough to take a candle. Fill any remaining gaps with more strands of moss.

RIGHT

A heart-shaped garland, conjuring up images of romance or fond memories, makes a perfect gift or keepsake. These garlands are made in exactly the same way as the round candle rings, but you need a heart-shaped wire as your starting point. You may be able to buy these ready-made, but if not you could make your own. Then all that is required is a hay rope (see page 151) wired to the heart, so that you have a firm base on which to glue the flowers — roses, bupleurum and lavender always make a delightful combination.

ABOVE

A dried artichoke sprayed with a glittering coat of gold paint is transformed into an elegant and unusual candleholder for a special occasion. Although the result is dramatic, the method is very simple. To fix the candle firmly in place (so that there is no danger of it wobbling or becoming a fire hazard), apply glue to the base of one of the ready-made candleholders you can buy from florists. Then push the candleholder firmly into the top of the artichoke. Cover the area around the candleholder with fresh green moss, glued into place. You could use a candle of any colour, but this red one (marked with tiny golden stars) creates just the right impact.

CAUTION — Do not leave burning candles unattended.

A COUNTRYSIDE DISPLAY

THIS WONDERFUL DESIGN REQUIRES MORE SKILL THAN YOU MIGHT EXPECT TO ACHIEVE ITS DELIBERATELY INFORMAL LOOK, WHICH WONDERFULLY EVOKES THE COUNTRYSIDE. THE REASON YOU NEED THE PIECE OF CARDBOARD IN THE BASE IS TO PREVENT ANY STUB (FLORAL) WIRES FROM BEING PUSHED THROUGH TO THE OUTER COVERING OF FABRIC. IF YOU PLAN TO TRIM THE HAY AT THE BOTTOM, CHOOSE MATERIAL TO MATCH THE SURROUNDING DECOR, OTHERWISE ANY FABRIC CAN BE USED.

YOU WILL NEED
dry foam block
fairly thick cardboard
fabric
mossing (floral) pins
reel (spool) wire
hay
selection of flowers such as alchemilla mollis, pink larkspur, marjoram, nigella orientalis, poppy heads, pink roses, wheat
stub (floral) wires
raffia (for trim)
knife
ruler and pencil
scissors
cutters

LEFT
A raffia bow tied round the base is an appropriate way to complete the display. Remember to put your finished creation where it will not be in direct sunlight.

1

Cut the foam block in half. Choose one piece (keeping the second for another display) and check that it has a square base, trimming the edges if necessary. Use the foam as a template to draw a square on the cardboard; then cut it out. Place the cardboard sandwiched on top of the piece of fabric and underneath the foam. If you are going to leave the sides exposed, the fabric needs to be large enough to cover the sides of the foam completely; if not, it needs to be a square about 2in (5cm) larger than the cardboard.

2

Fold the fabric up around the foam and use mossing (floral) pins to hold it in place, turning the corners and smoothing so that there are no wrinkles.

3

Wrap reel (spool) wire 3–4 times round the fabric-covered foam to make a firm starting point. Then begin to add the hay to form a collar around the sides. Keep the wire as tight as possible so that the hay stays in place. Cover the sides completely and secure the end of the wire by tying it to a mossing (floral) pin pushed into the base. Trim the hay at the base so that it is even and remove any straggly strands. If you want some of the fabric base to show, trim the hay about halfway up the sides of the block.

4

Separate the flowers into bunches and trim the stems. They need to be long enough for about 2in (5cm) to be pushed into the foam, while allowing ▶

the flower heads to show above the hay. Wire the flowers into small bunches of mixed or single varieties (see page 150). Then start to fill the space inside the hay collar with flowers, leaving no gaps. Try to make the centre a little higher and lean the bunches nearest the edge slightly outwards. Although the overall shape is square, the bunches should be at varying heights to help keep an informal feel to the display. With careful positioning, you can make a few stems of wheat look as if they are growing out of the hay.

RIGHT

Sometimes a design looks satisfactory when it is finished but needs a little extra something to make it look just right. Where and how you choose to display an arrangement can make all the difference. Included in this mix of flowers and foliage are achillea ptarmica, catkins, nigella, nigella orientalis, nicandra, oregano, poppy heads and roses — all of which combine to give a glorious sense of the country.

BELOW

Any mix of flowers surrounded by a collar of hay is an immediate reminder of the countryside. This display includes bupleurum, eucalyptus, white larkspur, lavender, oregano, peonies and pale pink roses. The raffia bow is tied at the back so that it looks tidy but still maintains a rustic appearance.

MAKING A TIED FLOWER STACK

DRIED GRASSES ARE THE MOST
TRADITIONAL INGREDIENTS FOR A STACK
BUT IT CAN BE EXTREMELY REWARDING
TO EXPERIMENT WITH FLOWERS, TWIGS
AND WHATEVER OTHER WOODY ITEMS
YOU CAN FIND. THE KEY TO SUCCESS IS
TO TAKE PLENTY OF TIME WHILE
ARRANGING THE STACK; ALTHOUGH
THEY SOMETIMES LOOK AS IF A HANDFUL
OF FLOWERS AND GRASSES HAVE BEEN
PLUCKED FROM THE COUNTRYSIDE,
STACKS REQUIRE THOUGHT, IF YOU ARE
TO ACHIEVE THE RIGHT BALANCE.

YOU WILL NEED
selection of flowers such as echinops,
pink larkspur, pink roses, poppy heads,
wheat
stub (floral) wire or reel (spool) wire
seagrass rope
cutters

LEFT
*A flower stack will bring welcome
warmth and colour to any room. Use
a few petals from one of the flowers in
the arrangement, or make a pile like
the poppy heads here, to marry the
display with its surroundings. Placing
the arrangement against a deep rich
background often helps to bring out
the strength of colours in individual
flowers. If you think that a display
looks out of place, try moving it to
another situation; a new environment
is often the answer.*

1

Separate all the flowers and foliage into piles so that they will be easy to work with. Trim any waste material from the stems. Select 2–3 stems of each variety to make a small bunch as the beginning of the stack; hold everything tightly in one hand. Initially, keep all the flower heads level.

2

Continue to add stems, but change the angle just a little every time you add more material to the stack. As you build up the shape, lower the flower heads slightly, so that they almost create a dome. When you have used all your flower supply, tie the bundle with a long stub (floral) wire or wind reel (spool) wire firmly around the stems about 5–6 times, so that they are as secure as possible. Trim the stems so that the stack stands on its own. Then add a seagrass rope — or one of raffia or fabric if you prefer — to conceal the wire underneath.

BELOW
A basket of fresh plums and nectarines placed beside a stack of dried flowers reveals the fruits of nature in perfect harmony. The materials in the stack are wired firmly together and the stems trimmed to make a steady base. Here, the main ingredients are carthamus, echinops, blue larkspur, lunaria, nigella and wheat — an unusual yet successful mix.

EXPERIMENTING WITH BOXES AND TUBS

AFTER A WHILE, WORKING WITH CONVENTIONAL POTS AND BASKETS MAY BECOME PREDICTABLE, IN WHICH CASE TRY CREATING DISPLAYS IN CARDBOARD BOXES, WOODEN TUBS OR ANY CONTAINERS THAT YOU THINK MIGHT BE APPROPRIATE. THESE EXPERIMENTAL DISPLAYS PROVIDE A GOOD OPPORTUNITY FOR USING UP ANY LEFT-OVER MATERIALS, BROKEN STEMS AND SO ON. BE BOLD WHEN YOU ARE EXPERIMENTING WITH NEW CREATIONS, AND REMEMBER THAT YOU CAN ALSO ACHIEVE EFFECTIVE RESULTS BY INCORPORATING ADDITIONAL ITEMS INTO A DISPLAY.

BELOW
In this arrangement, a cardboard box is simply quartered and single ingredients used to fill each area for dramatic contrast in colour and aroma. Lavender, poppy heads, roses and cinnamon sticks contrast with the moss ball (see pages 74–75).

LEFT

This luscious display includes peonies and pink larkspur, loosely packed into a box, tied with a green ribbon. Seed pods and fungi with interesting shapes provide additional elements in the display. The art of working successfully with designs like this is to know when to stop. The temptation is to keep adding materials but, if you are not careful, this can result in it looking crowded or overworked.

ABOVE, LEFT AND RIGHT

These two unusual displays are made with combinations of the same materials but use different containers: both are cardboard boxes, one covered with hessian (burlap) and the other painted green and trimmed with a piece of string. The materials (all glued in place) include echinops, gum pods, reindeer moss, fungi, willow sticks, cloves of garlic and seashells. Do not leave burning candles unattended.

LEFT

This antique pine tub is filled with a wonderfully rich mix of flowers, packed loosely without the aid of dry foam or wiring. The tub has a lively colour scheme, which includes pink larkspur and dark blue echinops. Wherever you decide to put a display, make sure that it will not be in direct sunlight, or the colours of the flowers will quickly fade.

A SUMMER TABLE SETTING

THIS WONDERFUL TABLE SETTING COMBINES THE BEST OF A COMPLETE RANGE OF VARYING SKILLS AND TECHNIQUES. CHAIRS ARE OFTEN FORGOTTEN WHEN IT COMES TO DECORATING THE TABLE AND SURROUNDINGS FOR A SPECIAL PARTY, BUT IT IS EXTREMELY EASY TO MAKE A SPRAY OF FLOWERS WHICH CAN BE ATTACHED TO THE CHAIR-BACKS. YOU MIGHT HAVE A PROBLEM TRYING TO FIND A SAFE FIXING FOR THE DISPLAYS, BUT IT IS FAIRLY STRAIGHTFORWARD IF THE CHAIRS HAVE HOLES IN THEIR BACKS. ALL YOU NEED TO DO IS TIE A STUB (FLORAL) WIRE THROUGH A HOLE, THEN PASS IT ROUND THE FINISHED DISPLAY, AND THEN BACK AGAIN THROUGH ANOTHER HOLE. BEND THE LOOSE ENDS OF WIRE INTO THE DISPLAY SO THAT THEY WILL NOT STICK INTO THE PERSON SITTING ON THE CHAIR.

YOU WILL NEED
selection of flowers such as alchemilla mollis, hydrangeas, larkspur, lavender, marjoram, nigella orientalis, oregano, peonies, pink roses
stub (floral) wires
fabric trim
cutters
pliers

LEFT
Among other varieties of flower, peonies, roses and lavender are used to decorate this chair, creating a combination which cannot fail to make an impact.

1

To decorate a chair back, first separate all the flowers into different piles and trim away any waste material. Try to work with as much space around you as possible. Ideally, spread the flowers out into a large semicircle, as this makes it easier to select the stems you want as you build the display.

2

Working on a flat surface, fan out a selection of 10–12 flowers, then add more to build up the shape and fill in the gaps. Make sure the flowers cover the whole area of the display. Gradually work downwards, so that flowers fill the whole area and cover the stems.

3

Once you are satisfied with the balance and shape of the display, slip a stub (floral) wire carefully around the back of the whole arrangement, about half-way down, and twist the wire firmly to hold the bunch together. Now you can pick up the display and, if necessary, add more flowers (held in place with wire). Make sure that none of the flower heads, especially those of roses or peonies, are buried by foliage or filler.

4

To complete the display, trim the ends of the stems to equal lengths — or leave them as they are if you prefer a staggered look — and tie a fabric ribbon in place to hide the wires holding the flowers together. Fix the arrangement with stub (floral) wires to the back of chair. If you accidentally damage any flower heads while you are tying the display in place, you can probably repair them or stick them back.

BELOW
One of the main advantages of working with dried materials is that you can create pieces weeks ahead of the date they are needed. You need plenty of preparation time to make all the elements in this summer table display, but adding mini-swags beside each place setting gives a really sumptuous feel to the party atmosphere. The method is exactly the same as that used for the Mixed Swag (see page 119) and to keep a consistency and balance across the table, the same ingredients were used as in the decoration for the chair-backs (see left for method). The centrepiece for the summer table display is a simple terracotta pot, filled with dry foam (see page 13) and crammed full with a glorious mix of flowers including peonies, lavender, pink roses, alchemilla mollis, nigella orientalis, marjoram and oregano. The display is kept quite low and compact, so that it will not block anyone's view or get in the way when everyone is sitting at the table. You can link the centrepiece to the mini-swags beside each place setting with a bed of moss, ivy or any similar fresh green foliage. Add candles in terracotta pots (see page 19) to complete the table (remember never to leave them burning unattended).

PLANTS AND MATERIALS

AS WITH MOST HOBBIES AND PROJECTS, THE MORE
FAMILIAR YOU ARE WITH THE RELEVANT TOOLS,
MATERIALS AND TECHNIQUES, THE EASIER THE TASK IN
HAND BECOMES. THIS CHAPTER PROVIDES USEFUL HINTS
WHICH WILL HELP YOU TO CREATE INSPIRATIONAL
DESIGNS AND TO ACQUIRE THE CONFIDENCE YOU NEED.

TOOLS AND EQUIPMENT

You will find it easier to create success-ful displays with dried materials if you use the appropriate equipment. You should be able to obtain the following basic items from good florists' shops or suppliers:

Candleholders These plastic fittings are available in a range of sizes. They have a star-shaped base which is easily pushed into dry foam to hold a candle.

Canes If you are creating a very large display, you need to extend the length of a stem by taping it to a cane. Canes can also be used to create a square or triangular frame for a garland, or to fix terracotta pots in a display.

Chicken wire This is a useful base for some displays (moss balls, for instance) and can also be used to hold flowers in large containers.

Copper or steel rings These in fact comprise two thin wire rings, which are used as the base for garlands. They are particularly useful if you plan to build a garland with heavy items.

Cutters A strong pair of spring-loaded cutters will cope with most material. Always use a pair that feels comfortable to work with. Some florists use strong scissors instead of cutters and you may find a pair adequate.

Dry foam This is usually grey or brown and available in rectangular blocks, spheres and cones. It is best to avoid foam that is intended for use with fresh flowers, because it tends to crumble if it is used with dried materials.

Florist's adhesive tape This is excellent for binding blocks of dry foam together. It can also be used to hold foam firmly in a container.

Florist's clear sealer A type of fixative, like a clear lacquer or very light varnish,

which is specifically for use on dried materials. When sprayed onto a display, it holds any loose material in place and will also help to keep it clean.

Glue gun This is an extremely useful tool which dramatically reduces the time needed to make a display (it is much faster to use glue than to wire materials). As with many things, better quality guns are more expensive. A gun with a trigger feed for the glue is easiest to use. Take care not to burn yourself.

Mossing (floral) pins These are ready-made pins which are used to hold mater-ial (usually moss, hence their name) in place.

Pliers Use these to secure and twist stub (floral) wires, chicken wire and so on.

Raffia Traditionally used by gardeners, this makes an attractive binding mater-ial, particularly if you are wanting to achieve a rustic look.

Reel (spool) wire This comes in a range of gauges and is essential for making swags and garlands. Experiment with different thicknesses until you find one with which you like working.

Scissors Sharp dressmakers' scissors

TOP
Whenever possible, use the specified tools and materials – it always makes a display much easier to create.

PREVIOUS PAGE AND ABOVE
The advantage with ready-made cane rings and fir cones is that they are fairly inexpensive and simple to use.

are best for cutting fabric or perhaps for trimming hay. As far as possible, resist using scissors to cut stems or the blades will quickly become blunt.

Setting clay This may be used to set trunks in pots for topiary displays or to hold down baskets so that they do not overbalance under the weight of a display.

String If you prefer, you can often substitute reel (spool) wire with string. The type used for gardening tends to be most suitable and comes in a range of brown and green colours that blend well with dried materials.

Stub (floral) wires These are available in different lengths and gauges; it is best to use wires that are as thick as you can comfortably work with and to buy long wire which you can cut to length as required. The heavier the material, the thicker the wire you will need to hold it in place.

CARE AND MAINTENANCE

How long a display of dried materials will last largely depends on the care that it receives. Above all, the golden rule is that a display should never be positioned so that it receives full sunlight. Even if it is exposed to the sun for as little as an hour a day, the material will quickly dry out and the colour will become bleached. The greens will fade first, soon followed by all the pastel shades, and before long the whole display will be a collection of muted browns. Even dyed material loses its colour in sunlight.

The second important rule is that displays should be kept dry and in a damp-free atmosphere, or the flowers will lose their vibrant colours, will possibly become mouldy and will begin to disintegrate. For this reason, it is best to avoid keeping displays in kitchens and bathrooms, unless the rooms are well ventilated and only high in humidity for short periods. If a display shows signs of a damp attack, you can save it by putting it immediately in a warm airing cupboard. You may possibly also be able to rescue a display simply by moving it to a warm room which has good ventilation.

If a display is kept dry and in a shaded position, it should last for at least a year, and in perfect conditions it might last for twice or three times as long. The display will certainly need to be cleaned and possibly repaired after the first year, if not before. To avoid getting dust everywhere, it is best to do the cleaning outside using a electric hairdryer (set on cold). Move the hairdryer backwards and forwards over the display and at the same time use a small soft paintbrush to help to clean away the dust. Some flowers will inevitably break from their stems during the cleaning, and the more delicate petals and leaves will probably snap off as well. This will not matter too much, provided that the display does not end up with large holes in it. If any gaps look obvious, you can fill them with new material. This is also the time to remove any elements that are no longer looking their best. Sometimes just replacing a few pieces will bring a new lease of life to an arrangement.

When the display is as clean as is possible, you can give it a further lift by spraying it with a liberal coat of florist's sealer. This will brighten the faded colours slightly, as well as helping to prevent a future build-up of dust. Alternatively, if you think the arrangement is too old to be displayed in its current state, but you cannot bear to throw it away, you can save it with a coat of paint. Spray paints which give a gentle frosting effect are available in a wide range of colours and can transform a display. Using just one colour often works particularly well. If you choose white paint, it will allow any natural colours remaining in the material to show through.

PROFESSIONAL HINTS

Whether you are making a simple pot of roses or a more complicated arrangement, there are a few basic techniques which make all the difference to the finished display. With practice, and as you become more experienced, all the following will become second nature but you may find some aspects a little fiddly when you first start to handle dried materials.

WIRING A BUNCH OF FLOWERS

This basic skill is integral to the art of working with dried flowers. Wired bunches are more secure than single stems (which are often too brittle or too thick to insert into dry foam) and also help to create density in an arrangement.

1

Take 4–6 stems cut to the length you require. Hold the stems firmly together with one hand and pass a stub (floral) wire behind them so that the wire and stems are at right angles to each other, forming a cross. Leave about 1½in (4cm) of the wire protruding at the top.

2

Hold the wire and stems together between your thumb and forefinger of one hand. With the other hand, bend the wire towards you, loop it around the stems and push it away from you.

3

Continue to hold the stems and wire together; pull the short end of wire up so it lies lengthways along the stems. Now wrap the longer length of wire 3–4 times around the stems to hold them together. The wire should be firm but not so tight that the stems break.

STEAMING ROSES

This simple technique can greatly improve the appearance of roses, although sometimes the central petals may be discoloured, so take care not to open them too much.

1

Bring an electric kettle of water to the boil. Hold the rose by its stem, head downwards, in the steam for a few seconds until the outside petals start to waver.

2

Immediately remove the rose from the steam and with a fingertip gently push back the petals to open them up. If necessary, return the rose briefly to the steam and repeat the procedure.

MAKING A HAY ROPE OR COLLAR

The method for making a rope or collar out of hay is exactly the same, except that the collar needs to be thicker and the two ends joined together to form a circle. As hay is both inexpensive and versatile, it is well worth mastering this basic technique. Hay ropes and collars make particularly useful starting points for many garlands and swags.

1

Take a good handful of hay and scrunch it up to form a sausage. Wind reel (spool) wire (or string or raffia) around this and tie in place. Twist the wire round the hay, leaving spaces of about ½in (1cm) between each twist. Keep adding more hay as you build up the length of rope. Make sure that the rope is firm and that the binding material is very tight. The hay should not give at all when you squeeze it.

2

Keep adding more hay, trying to keep the width of the rope even, until you have made the required length. If you are making a rope for use in a swag, it need only be about ¼in (5mm) in diameter. For a garland or a very large swag, the diameter needs to be about 1in (2.5cm). Whatever you are making, pack the hay as firmly as possible to make a good base for the decorative materials that you will be using. Once you have completed the rope or collar, trim away any loose hay and ensure that the end of the binding material is securely fastened.

TYING A PAPER BOW

Sometimes a display needs a ribbon to add just the right finishing touch. Fabric can work well occasionally but paper ribbon is particularly effective because it holds its shape. It is also extremely easy to work with.

1

Cut the length of ribbon you require (if necessary, calculate roughly how much you need by going through the motions of tying a imaginary bow). Gently tease the ribbon open so that it is completely flat. Then scrunch the ribbon up again.

2

Fold the length in half and pull down the centre to make an M-shape.

3

Holding the two loops, cross them over each other, tie them into a knot and pull tightly. Adjust the size of the bow as necessary by pulling on the tails.

4

Open out the ribbon so that the bow is well rounded. Fix the bow to the display with a dab of glue or with a stub (floral) wire or reel (spool) wire threaded through the back of the knot.

CONTAINERS

More often than not, the container in which you choose to make your display is the key to success. Baskets, in particular, go well with dried materials but, whatever you select, it is essential that a basket suits the intended design – never make do with something that is inappropriate. For instance, the baskets that florists sometimes incorporate in fresh flower displays are not meant to be kept after the arrangement has died, and are rarely suitable for displays with dried materials.

If you find a basket with a wonderful colour and texture, try to make the basket a main feature in the display and emphasize its qualities. On the other hand, if you have an old basket that is past its best, you may be able to disguise any flaws, perhaps by covering it with moss, or by arranging material so that it hangs well over the sides. Remember that the appearance of some baskets can be improved if you remove the handles, or if you spray the baskets with paint.

Before you use a basket, make sure that there are no hidden bugs in the base which might infest either the materials in the display or your furniture. Wash baskets so they are completely clean and check for any holes in the basketwork. If a basket does have bore holes and you still want to use it, treat it first with a pesticide. Follow the manufacturer's instructions and leave it to dry thoroughly before you start on your design. If you plan to stand the finished display on a polished surface, it might be wise to place it on a mat, to ensure there is no chance of damage from traces of pesticide. Similarly, take care that no sharp pieces are sticking out from the bottom of a basket – they might damage the surface underneath. If you are determined to use a basket

that is in bad condition, you should be able to improve its appearance and partly restore it to its original colour by applying a good-quality wax (use a soft brush).

Baskets are the most frequently used type of container for display work, but other materials are equally suitable. Terracotta pots make an excellent base for many displays, and designs using these can be easily adapted to suit other containers. Wherever possible, however, try to avoid anything with a small neck (which makes it very difficult to produce a balanced display). Above all, if you want to use a container that is special to you, remember that the safest option is to build the display in another (inexpensive and replaceable) container, which you can then put inside your chosen container without any fear of breakage.

When hunting for unusual or different containers, remember that the kitchen can be a surprisingly fruitful source – you can often find something suitable at

ABOVE

Any type of container can be used to hold a display. However, if you plan to use something made of glass, place a piece of dry foam in the centre of the container, and then pack pot pourri or quantities of moss around the foam, so that none of the workings will be visible.

the back of a cupboard. Similarly, garden sheds can sometimes yield just what is needed. If you are using a copper or brass container, build the display in something else if you are going to polish the container regularly, although ultimately you may decide that a matt surface gives the display a more pleasing appearance. Leaving a pot or container outdoors for a short while will allow it to weather so that it gains a naturally distressed look. This is especially appropriate for decorative wire baskets – be sure to coat these with wax before use (this will seal the surface and bring out the colour of the wire).

POPULAR DRIED MATERIALS

The range of dried flowers and materials available for use in displays is enormous. Some items can easily be grown in your garden while others can only be obtained from good florists or suppliers. Although the materials are dried, check that they are from fresh stock and free from dust and moths before buying. The following are among the most popular varieties used by professionals today.

Achillea filipendulina Golden yarrow
This mustard yellow plant has been a favourite for many years. The large head fills spaces quickly and seems to be a necessity for any large country-style arrangement. This achillea is easy to keep dust-free – the heads will withstand cleaning with a soft brush and a hairdryer.

Achillea ptarmica The Pearl
These clusters of small bright white flowers on dark green stems need to be used with care, as the bright white tends to stand out when combined with other materials. Achillea has a long life but needs to be kept away from damp or the white will turn pale brown very quickly.

Alchemilla mollis Lady's mantle
This is a beautiful material to use; it can be added to all types of display and gives a soft feel to an arrangement. However, in time, the colour will fade to a soft yellow brown. Take care when using, as it tends to break quite readily. Alchemilla is very easy to grow.

Amaranthus Love-lies-bleeding
This is most commonly available either in its natural dark green state or dyed dark red. Amaranthus may be long and upright but is also available in the shape of a long soft tail. Be selective when choosing bunches as its thickness and length vary tremendously. For small display work, it is much better to use a thinner variety.

Ambrosinia
Widely available in two versions – one short and one long – this pale green plant has a wonderful scent that is especially strong when it is being worked with. As is the case with all green material, avoid placing ambrosinia in strong light if you want to maintain its colour for as long as possible. If the display is in a centrally heated house, it will tend to drop as it dries out and if it is knocked, so put it somewhere out of the the way.

Anaphalis margaritacea Pearl everlasting
This fluffy white flower is extremely easy to grow; the flowers will dry in the garden while on the stem. Make sure you pick them before they start to go to seed or you will have a room full of fluff. The greeny yellow centre sits well beside other materials.

Banksia serrata Holly oak
This very large leaf is usually sold in a preserved form. It makes a good substitute for holly, is a good filler for a large display and should not lose its shape or dry out. It can also be sprayed with paint to make a perfect colour match or gilded lightly with gold for a winter decoration.

Bupleurum griffiti
This plant is a useful filler, but its green colour will fade fast if it is exposed to too much light. Each stem has a large quantity of heads, each with a collection of small seeds.

Carthamus Safflower or saffron thistle
Two main varieties are available – with and without flowers. The dark ginger flower is often used to make dye and it makes a stunning addition to a display. Commercial bunches tend to be fairly large, so they need to be split and wired.

Choose only flowers with deep green leaves and dark orange flowers (these indicate that the stock is fresh).

Consolida Larkspur
Very close to the delphinium, these flowers come in a range of colours but are usually blue, pink or white. If the flowers are faded, the stock has probably been around for a while. Any bunches that are a little crushed can be revived by gently steaming them over a kettle. Larkspur is among the most useful display flowers.

Cynara scolymus Globe artichoke
If you can bear not to eat these wonderful plants, they are well worth drying. Either in full bloom or when they are quite small, they can make a huge statement and they deserve to be displayed alone in a large vase. The outside comes in a range of green and purple colours and, when in full bloom, the centre is a mass of delicate mauve fronds. To dry them at home, hang them upside down, wrapped in paper and with the bottom open, over a constant flow of warmth. They will take 2–3 weeks to dry.

Echinops ritro Blue; Miniature or globe thistle
When they are at their best, the globe-shaped heads are a deep steely blue. Always handle echinops with care as they are prone to break apart (fresh ones are less likely to be damaged). Although they are quite expensive to buy, they are easy to grow in the right conditions.

Echinops sphaerocephalus Silver
This belongs to the same family as the blue echinops but is a much larger variety, which comes in a range of delicate blues and greens. It takes spray colour very well, so it is useful for Christmas decorations or for displays that need something different. Handle echinops with care as the flower heads are very spiky.

Eryngium planum Sea holly
This plant, which comprises clusters of small blue thistles, needs to be handled with care (it is advisable to wear gloves). Although it is very spiky, this blue plant lasts for a long time and looks dramatic. As it fades, it becomes grey/green turning to a pale brown.

Eucalyptus spiralus Eucalyptus
Available mostly as a preserved product, this wonderful leaf normally comes in two colours, green and brown. It is a joy to work with, as it gives off a beautiful scent when the stems and leaves are bruised (this fragrance lasts for months). Eucalyptus is ideal for large displays that require long stems.

Fagus sylvatica Copper beech
This dark brown leaf provides an extremely good backdrop when combined with any number of other dried materials. It can be used in its natural condition collected from the woods, although the leaves tend to curl as they dry. When used as a preserved material, it will keep for an indefinite period.

Helianthus Sunflower
These large yellow flowers are well known but have only recently become available as dried materials on a commercial basis. The yellow petals are usually quite small and have a tendency to fade; nevertheless, the flowers are useful in large displays. If necessary, the height of the sunflowers can easily be extended by pushing a cane into the hollow of each flower-stem or by wiring a cane to a stem.

Helichrysum Strawflower or everlasting flower
This is one of the best-known dried flowers and it has slipped from favour with many arrangers. However, it still has a firm place on the dried material list and should not be neglected. The range of colours available is vast and the flower-head has a very long life. It is best

when used in bunches, rather than as single flowers, to give a stunning patch of colour.

Hydrangea macrophylla Hydrangea
This is one of the most useful of dried materials. Its colours range from very dark pink through to an almost pale grey and a variety of tones to dark blue. Hydrangeas can be dried very easily at home in a dark warm place. The large heads will quickly fill a display and they have a long life.

Lavandula stoechas French lavender
This variety is a magnificent blue – its rich colour is outstanding and it has a delightful perfume. Take care when buying as the quality often varies. A vast range of lavender is available; a paler variety is also very useful for dried arrangements.

Limonium suworowii Rat's tail statice
These dark to pale pink flowers come in a huge variety of lengths. Although most stems will be fairly straight when fresh, they tend to drop after a time in a display. They look their best when used in small bunches rather than single stems and will bring a change of texture

Mentha Mint
This pale purple flower looks very uninspiring when viewed alone but, when combined with other materials, it makes a good partner. It also gives off a lovely mint scent when the leaves and stems are cut. Stalks can also be used in a display to add to the scent.

Nicandra physalodes Apple-of-Peru, shoo-fly plant
This green seed pod makes a useful alternative to orange physalis (Chinese lanterns). Its subtle colouring can be used with many different ingredients and its shape provides an unusual texture. Like all green plants, nicandra does not like bright light so keep it away from direct sunlight. In time, the green will turn a dark brown (for a seed pod this is quite acceptable).

Nigella damascena Love-in-a-mist
A real favourite, these purple and green seed pods have an unusual shape. However, they dislike bright light and will fade very fast unless kept in shade. Nigella is particularly useful for special occasion displays where the colour can be enhanced or changed with spray paints (gold or silver at Christmas, for instance).

Nigella orientalis
This is a variation of love-in-a-mist; it comes from the same family but is a completely different shape (spiky rather than rounded). Another all-green plant, it is susceptible to loss of colour but its unusual shape makes up for this. It is frequently more difficult to obtain than love-in-a-mist.

Origanum marjorana Marjoram
This resembles the herb oregano but has no flavour when dried. Its dark purple and green colour works well with most materials, however, especially roses, peonies, nigella and lavender.

Origanum vulgare Oregano
This much-loved herb makes an excellent dried plant. It has a very unusual texture and also releases a beautiful scent. The colour will keep indefinitely, and it is certainly one of the more robust plants. Any unused pieces can be kept to form part of a pot pourri; it mixes well with lavender and roses.

From top left to bottom right: *Achillea filipendulina, Achillea ptarmica* (Lilac Beauty), *Achillea ptarmica* (The Pearl), *Alchemilla mollis, Amaranthus, Amaranthus* (dyed red), *Ambrosinia, Anaphalis margaritacea, Banksia serrata, Bupleurum griffiti, Carthamus, Consolida, Cynara scolymus, Echinops ritro* Blue, *Echinops sphaerocephalus* Silver, *Helianthus, Helichrysum, Laurus nobilis* (bay leaves), *Lavandula stoechas, Limonium suworowii.*

Paeonia Peony

Although these are a little expensive to buy – and only in season for a short while – they are quite easy to air-dry at home. Most peonies are dark pink but they can also be a rich pinky cream. A note of caution: moths love peonies so make sure that there are no eggs in the flowers before you bring them indoors, or you will find that any available fabric will be infested with moths in no time.

Papaver Poppy seed head

These seed pods can make a welcome addition to almost any display. Coloured from a dark powder grey through to green/grey, they will suit most colourways. Avoid spraying the pods with a clear lacquer, because this will destroy their powder bloom that is such an attractive feature.

Physalis Chinese lantern

This paper-thin orange favourite is a well-used material but it still deserves a mention. The vivid orange colour will not last if exposed to strong light. Physalis is fairly easy to grow in the garden although you will probably not have as many seed pods on home-grown varieties as on commercial types.

Protea compacta Cape honey flower

This woody head will last for ever and needs only an occasional dusting to maintain its good looks. A range of different sizes is available. If you want to cut the stems, you will need a strong pair of cutters.

Quercus Oak

This leaf is used in a similar way to preserved copper beech, although the leaf tends to be a little thicker and should also last for longer. In its preserved state, oak often has a little brown dye added, which helps to give the leaves a dark rich lasting colour.

Rosa Rose

A wide range of different colours is available, and although roses are among the most expensive of dried flowers, they are frequently also the most exquisite. Always save them until last so that the rose heads do not become broken while constructing the display. Most varieties will welcome a little steaming to ease the shape and increase the size – it releases a beautiful scent as well. Roses are prone to attack from moths, so inspect them for eggs from time to time. If you find any, throw the flowers out immediately or moths will soon be attacking your fabric.

Rosa paleander

These are the mini versions of the standard dried roses. One of their main advantages is that they are not generally prone to moth attack. They are also available in a huge range of colours. Watch out for the thorns, which are particularly vicious. Combined with larger roses these look particularly good in a display.

Sanfordii

These small clusters of bright yellow flowers make a striking addition to any display. The golden yellow has a long life although the flower heads need to be supported by other materials or the weight of the flowers tends to bend the stems, which can look ugly.

Silene pendula Campion

This tiny pink flower looks as though it is fresh. It will lose some of the petals as it is worked with but not enough to spoil the finished result. The colour keeps for a long time and the small flower heads create a soft look to a display. You will probably need to support the heads with wire to stop them from hanging down.

Solidaster

This pale yellow flower keeps its colour well. It normally comes in fairly large bunches which go a long way. Each stem has dozens of flowers that can be wired into small bunches. Solidaster makes a good filler flower, as an alternative to bupleurum, for instance.

Tagetes erecta Marigold

Whether bright yellow or orange, this makes a spectacular splash of colour in any display. Choose flowers with as little damage as possible. They look almost fresh and can even be arranged alone in a terracotta pot with stunning results.

Triticum tarwe Wheat

This is one of a number of grasses available. Although grasses are very attractive, they need to be used with care. Also, they contain large amounts of chlorophyll so their green colour is short-lived. Grasses have largely been responsible for giving display work a bad reputation (until recently many people could only see dried materials as brown and boring) so use grasses with care.

Xeranthemum Immortelle

These small star-shaped flowers are mostly purple or white. They have an extremely long shelf life (which is why they are sometimes referred to as 'everlastings') and they tolerate bright light well. Often used as a filler because they are inexpensive, immortelles should be used with care or their strong purple colour will dominate a display.

From top left to bottom right: *Mentha, Nicandra physalodes, Nigella damascena, Nigella orientalis, Origanum vulgare, Origanum marjorana, Paeonia, Papaver, Physalis, Picea pungens* (blue pine or spruce), *Protea compacta, Rosa* (six varieties), *Rosmarinus* (rosemary), *Silene pendula, Triticum tarwe.*

ABOVE
A basket filled to the brim with a selection of nuts provides a simple, effective arrangement.

ABOVE RIGHT
Fir cones and seed pods of varying shapes and sizes provide a welcome contrast in texture to most displays of dried materials.

RIGHT
Dried fungi and lichens of all types can give a remarkable lift to most displays. Fungi will frequently be found on sale with stems ready-fixed so that they can easily be added to an arrangement. If yours have no stems, you will need to add them. This is best done with a glue gun. Dried fungi also benefit from a light spray of florist's clear sealer which brings out the rich dark woody colours.

SUPPLIERS

There are numerous stockists of dried materials, but the following are recommended as being particularly reliable suppliers of good quality dried flowers. In time, you may find that a supplier changes direction and does not stock the range that you require. All the materials you need to make the designs in this book can be obtained from Terence Moore Designs, which also undertakes special commissions and runs one-day workshops for individuals and groups.

When buying dried stock, make sure that it is as fresh as possible and has plenty of colour. If the material looks muddy or is brittle to touch, then it has been in stock for longer than is desirable and should be avoided. Suppliers who stock only a small range of dried materials will probably have a slow turnover, so you should avoid buying from them – unless, of course, they have exactly what you are looking for.

UNITED KINGDOM

Terence Moore Designs
The Barn Workshop, Burleigh Lane
Crawley Down, West Sussex RH10 4LF
Tel./Fax: (0342) 717944

The Bay Tree Florist
19 Upper High Street, Thame, Oxon
OX9 3EX
Tel: (0844) 217993

Bright Ideas
38 High Street, Lewes, East Sussex
BN7 2LU
Tel: (0273) 474395

Country Style
358 Fulwood Road, Ranmoor, Sheffield
S10 3GD
Tel: (0742) 309067

De La Mares Florist
Rue A Don, Grouville, Jersey
Channel Islands
Tel: (0534) 851538

Forsyths
7 Market Place, St Albans, Herts
AL3 5DK
Tel: (0727) 839702

Hilliers Garden Centre
London Road (A30), Windlesham
Surrey GU20 6LN
Tel: (0344) 23166

Hilliers Garden Centre
Woodhouse Lane, Botley, Southampton
SO3 2EZ
Tel: (0489) 782306

Lesley Hart Dried Flowers
37 Smith Street, Warwick CV34 4JA
Tel: (0926) 490356

Mews Gallery
Old Stone House, 23 Killenchy
Comber, Co. Down, Northern Ireland
BT23 5AP
Tel: (0247) 874044

Page and Bolland
Denscombe Mill, Shillingford, Tiverton
Devon EX16 9BH
Tel: (0398) 6283

Three French Hens
Home Farm, Swinfen, Nr Lichfield
Staffs WS14 9QR
Tel: (0543) 481613

UNITED STATES

American Oaks Preserving Company, Inc.
601 Mulberry Street, North Judson
Indiana, 46366
Tel: (800) 348–5008; Call for local retailers.

Earthstar Herb Gardens
438 West Perkinsville Road
China Valley, Arizona, 86323
Tel: (602) 636 2565; Catalog $1.00.

Fischer & Page, Ltd.
134 West 28th Street, New York
NY 10001 (wholesale).

Gold Mine Catalog
W10635, Highway 1, Reeseville
Wisconsin, 53579
Tel: (414) 927–3603; Catalog $2.00.

Herb Gathering
5742 Kenwood, Kansas City
Missouri, 64110
Tel: (816) 523-2653; Catalog $2.00 (refundable).

J&T Imports
P.O. Box 642, Solana Beach, California
92075 (wholesale).

LeeWards
Main Office, Elgin, Illinois, 60120
Tel: (708) 888-5800; Call for local retailers.

Meadow Everlasting
R.R. 1, 149 Shabbona Road, Malta
Illinois, 60150
Tel: (815) 825, 2539; Catalog $1.00.

Patchogue Florals Fantasyland
10 Robinson Avenue, East Patchogue
New York, 11772
Tel: (516) 475–2059.

Stamens & Pistils
875 Third Avenue, New York, NY 10022
Tel: (212) 593–1888

Sun Kempt
P.O. Box 231, Yorkviller, NY 13495
Tel: (315) 797–9618; Catalog $1.00 (refundable).

Tom Thumb Workshop
Rt. 13, Box 357, Mappsville
Virginia, 23407
Tel: (804) 824–3507; Catalog $1.00.

Wayside Gardens
1 Garden Lane, Hodges, South Carolina
29695–0001
Tel: (800) 845–1124; Free catalog.

Well-Sweep Herb Farm
317 Mount Bethel Road, Port Murray
New Jersey, 07865
Tel: (201) 852–5390; Catalog $1.00.

CANADA

Crafts Canada
440-28 Street, NE, Calgary
Alberta T2A 6T3
Tel: (403) 569–2355

Multi-Crafts and Gifts
2210 Thurston Drive, Ottawa
Ontario, K1G 5L5

INDEX

AKNOWLEDGEMENTS

This book could not have been created without the help of a number of people. First, my thanks are due to Karen, without whom we could not have completed everything on time. I also owe a big thank-you to my wife, Suzy, whose excellent organizational skills allowed me to work on this project while she kept the business running smoothly. My thanks are also due to Nicholas and William for the time they allowed me to write in peace; to Ian and Andrea, John and Veronica, John Warner for their support; and to Tony and Jenny, for the loan of their conservatory when the weather would not allow Michelle Garrett to take her wonderfully inspiring photographs outdoors. A special thank-you too to Joanna for her faith in me, and Nicky who worked so hard.